FOREWORD

In any conceptualization of instructional leadership, the task of teacher supervision must be included. This third edition on clinical supervision affords an up-to-date account of the state of the art with a detailed analysis of the carefully conceived stages of this process. It offers practitioners and scholars alike a *practical, user-friendly* design on the clinical supervision process and promises to be an important book as the supervisory relationship with teachers matures.

Robert Anderson and Robert Krajewski have labored in the supervision vineyard for many years. As teachers and scholars in the field, they bring a unique, rich experience to this book which probes deeply into the delicate interpersonal relationship which must be cultivated if a climate of mutual trust and respect is to prevail between the teacher and supervisor.

That this relationship is delicate has always been known. As schools and systems grew larger in size over the last several decades, many abuses developed in the supervisory relationship. Only now are we realizing the significance of working with teachers in the manner(s) this book suggests.

This book makes an enormous contribution to the entire field of instructional leadership. As we witness the continued press for quality in the schools, the demand for *instructional leadership* from both line and staff personnel is increasing. What are the tasks involved in such leadership?

I believe the building principals who would be called *instructional* leaders would spend at least half or more of their time engaged in the following activities: (1) curriculum planning, (2) clinical supervision, (3) staff development, and (4) teacher evaluation.

Current evidence suggests that many principals spend approximately 15 percent of their time in all four activities *combined*. They are compelled to spend considerable time in discipline, operations, parental communication, and other activities. The instructional supervision task is

frequently avoided simply because principals are not comfortable with it. Moreover, teachers are increasingly becoming involved in the "helping relationship" with their colleagues, and thus will be more effective in such new roles if they fully understand clinical supervision.

Staff-level supervisors also need to understand the concept of clinical supervision and the skill of leadership if they are to provide a vision of leadership for the school which is motivational in nature and supports a successful learning environment. This book lays out the deep feelings many teachers have about supervision. Knowledge of these feelings must be understood and dealt with if a mature and helping relationship is to prevail. This book also provides the knowledge base critical for effective supervision.

The clinical supervision movement will be assisted by the work presented in this book. The movement has come a long way from the early conceptualization of Morris Cogan and subsequent refinement of Robert Goldhammer. Both Anderson and Krajewski contribute greatly in assuring that the complexities of the supervisory relationship are better understood and incorporated into practice. I recommend this book as essential reading for neophyte and experienced supervisors.

GORDON CAWELTI
Executive Director Emeritus
Association for Supervision and Curriculum Development
Alexandria, Virginia

CHAPTER

1

THEORY INTO PRACTICE

In This Chapter

- Clinical Supervision Defined
- A Scenario: Conversation in the Coffee Shop
- A Second Scenario: The Practitioners Speak
- Summary

This chapter attempts to build a bridge between theory and practice. It begins with definitions of clinical supervision by supervision experts. It then presents a scenario with the authors, another college professor, and five of the authors' former graduate students discussing the changing role of clinical supervision. Next is presented the results of a seven-item narrative response from selected teachers, principals, and supervisors throughout the country on the use of clinical supervision in schools. Lastly, a summary dialogue of this response provides a transition to the qualities to be discussed in Chapter 2.

CLINICAL SUPERVISION DEFINED

■ Morris Cogan, the first person to develop and define clinical supervision, described it as:

> the rationale and practice designed to improve the teacher's classroom performance. It takes its principal data from the events of the classroom. The analysis of these data and the relationship between the teacher and supervisor form the basis of the program, procedures, and strategies designed to improve the students' learning by improving the teacher's classroom behavior.[1]

Sergiovanni and Starratt say that clinical supervision:

> refers to face-to-face contact with teachers with the intent of improving instruction and increasing professional growth. In many respects, a one-to-one correspondence exists between improving classroom instruction and increasing professional growth, and for this reason staff development and clinical supervision are inseparable concepts and activities.[2]

Acheson and Gall indicate that:

> clinical supervision has as its goal the professional development of teachers, with an emphasis on improving teachers' classroom performance. It is supervision to help the teacher improve his or her instructional performance.[3]

Flanders sees clinical supervision as:

> a special case of teaching in which at least two persons are concerned with the improvement of teaching and at least one of the individuals is a teacher whose performance is to be studied. . . . [I]t seeks to stimulate some change in teaching, to show that a change did, in fact, take place, and to compare the old and new patterns of instruction in ways that will give a teacher useful insights into the instructional process.[4]

Lovell and Wiles define clinical supervision as:

> a problem solving approach to instructional supervision in which objective observation and analysis of teaching is the basis for feedback as frameworks for change and improvement of performance.[5]

Snyder defines clinical supervision as "a useful management and supervisory tool for observing teaching" and as "an observation system which supervisors and principals use in gathering data on teaching performance."[6]

Daresh notes that "clinical supervision is best viewed as a collegial practice, not as something that a superordinate . . . does to a teacher, but as a peer-to-peer activity."[7]

Beach and Reinhartz state that "clinical supervision is a long-term field-based process that has been called 'supervision up close' because it brings clarity to the classroom and seeks to upgrade the quality of instruction."[8]

Oliva states that:

> clinical supervision is the provision of supervisory help to the individual teacher to improve instruction. The typical clinical model calls for a one-to-one, face-to-face relationship between the teacher and supervisor. Clinical supervision focuses on the events that take place in the classroom.[9]

Glickman regards clinical supervision to be direct human assistance to teachers.[10]

These and other definitions have several elements in common, such as classroom data, observation, and improvement of teaching. Our own definition is consistent to a significant extent with all of them, and in a sense enhances the common elements. We feel it extends these definitions and further points to a cycle or system in which clinical supervision operates.

As we see it, then, clinical supervision (CS) is *that aspect of instructional supervision which draws upon data from first-hand observation of actual teaching, or other professional events, and involves face-to-face and other associated interactions between the observer(s) and the person(s) observed in the course of analyzing the observed professional behaviors and activities and seeking to define and/or develop next steps toward improved performance.*

A SCENARIO: CONVERSATION IN THE COFFEE SHOP

■ It is the morning of the second and final day of the annual fall conference of a large state affiliate unit of the Association for Supervision and Curriculum Development (ASCD). The third general session of the conference has just ended on a high note, and we (Bob Krajewski and Bob Anderson) sit in the coffee shop of the Hyatt Regency Hotel along with Lee, a professor from nearby State U., and five of our former graduate students: Karen, an assistant elementary-school principal; Roosevelt, a high-school principal; Maria, a middle-school teacher; Barbara, team leader in an intermediate-grades unit; and John, an assistant superintendent for curriculum and instruction. We happen to be seated near the hotel's events board, which reads:

TODAY'S EVENTS

9–10:30 AM	Third General Session Restructuring and Transforming American Schools	Cascade Ballroom A-B-C
10:30–11 AM	Social and Break	Lobby
11 AM–Noon	*Breakout Sessions*	
	Peer Coaching/Peer Supervision	Crystal A
	Site-based Management	Crystal B
	Teacher Empowerment	Diamond
	Interdisciplinary Teaming	Shenandoah
	Cooperative Learning	Buccaneer
	Higher Order Thinking Skills	Horizon A
	Multicultural Dimensions	Emerald
	School/University Partnerships	Ivory
1:30–3:30 PM	School Visits (sign up in Lobby)	
4:30–6 PM	President's Address	Cascade A-B
	Business Meeting	Cascade C

Yesterday, we (Krajewski and Anderson) presented a special section, "Clinical Supervision: Nurturing Rapport." Karen, who helped with the simulation aspect of the section, opens the conversation as we await coffee and sweet rolls.

Karen: *(to both Bobs)* I thought our session yesterday went very well, except for that newspaper reporter who couldn't buy into the concept of mutual vulnerability.

Bob K: Yeah, she seemed to think that the boss should always be and act like the boss. I hope she attends the 11 o'clock session in Crystal A—it might do her some good.

Roosevelt: I wish I could attend every one of the breakout sessions.

Barbara: Me, too. They all seem very appropriate to my needs and interests at the moment.

Bob A: Whoever planned this day of the program really understood how all these topics and themes complement one another. With yesterday's stuff on curriculum and supervision, and today's restructuring material, it's been a really good summary of the changing scene.

Maria: Bob [A], which of the 11 o'clock sections relates most closely to your ideas on clinical supervision?

Bob A: That's a tough call to make. They all do, even the school/university part. *(Looks at Lee.)*

Lee: I agree with that. At State U. we're trying to make better connections with the schools on all of these dimensions, especially in the in-service and staff development areas. We're finding that clinical supervision activities in the schools open the door to all kinds of thinking about coaching, empowerment, school culture, and so on.

John: Lee, you may remember that it was that workshop that Bob Krajewski offered on your campus five years ago—or was it six?—that got our central office people all fired up about helping principals with their instructional leadership skills. You, and some of your professor colleagues, have been great about coming in and working with us.

Lee: Yes, and we've learned a lot, too. And there's more to learn. I'm going to the Crystal A session in a few minutes.

Bob K: That's great. It should be an important session.

Roosevelt: But, Bob [K], as I recall that 1984 workshop, you weren't all that hot on peer coaching, were you? Yesterday you seemed like a real advocate. Have you changed your mind?

Bob K: No. Bob [A] and I have always talked about clinical supervision as both content and process. Collaboration and collegiality have always been integral components of the CS process. Peer coaching is a good supplement—

Bob A: Change that to "excellent" supplement.

Bob K: Okay, it's an excellent supplement to the traditional CS model. Or perhaps it's even an excellent example of it.

Karen: So, now you're talking teacher-to-teacher supervision. Is this now the big deal?

BARBARA: No, we don't want to forget about the importance of *everyone's* role in clinical supervision. As a team leader, which I suppose means that I'm teacher-to-teacher when I supervise or coach, I feel that I'm also in a leader-type role. That's okay, isn't it?

BOB A: Of course it's okay. But let's not get hung up on role. If we look at the concept of clinical supervision, with its emphasis on stimulating growth, almost anybody can be the beneficiary, and, similarly, everybody can play the role of helper, or mediator, or facilitator, or whatever we choose to call the person at the other end of the dialogue. There's a person being helped (and, John and Roosevelt, as you know, a school administrator needs supervisory help also) and a person doing the helping.

BOB K: In our definition, then, whenever it says "supervisor," we probably should explain that it means the helper, and whenever it says "teacher," it could be referring to all sorts of "helpees"—teachers, principals, supervisors, team leaders . . .

LEE: And professors!

BOB A: Buy the professor a beer! When university people talk that way, we're really making progress.

MARIA: I really like your idea that CS is not just a top-to-bottom or authoritarian activity. I felt rather pushed around by the Hunter stuff we used to have. I enjoyed the contrast yesterday when you two Bobs were saying that the teacher's perceived needs should be the focus.

JOHN: Except, of course, when the teacher is in trouble.

MARIA: Yes, I understand that. But most teachers aren't really in trouble, they're just trying to get better. And I like it when my superior, or my teammates, base their observations on topics or problems that I help to identify.

BOB A: Well, you know, Bob [K] and I have been thinking about how CS has been changing—you might say growing up—over the past dozen or so years, and we're pleased that Maria's observation is being respected more and more. It's wonderful that the colleagues of teachers (peers, as they say) are playing a major role in instructional improvement through the use of the CS observation cycle or variants thereof.

LEE: Will this idea be prominent in the third edition you're working on?

BOB A: Hell, yes! I think that peer supervision, or peer coaching, as many call it, was always at least implicit in the early CS models, but now we have explicated its importance. You may or may not know that when Morris Cogan first developed the approach, it was for the purpose of providing groups of Harvard student teachers the opportunity to observe and give feedback to one another. The Harvard–Newton Summer Program was begun in 1955 to provide a quick student-teaching experience for future intern teachers. Cogan

(in the secondary program) and I (in the elementary program) saw great value in having the student teachers (usually four or five in each class) observe and critique each other. Then in 1960, when I started the Harvard–Lexington Summer Program to help experienced teachers and administrators to learn more about team teaching, Cogan and his student Bob Goldhammer were the supervision kingpins, and the observation cycle was done by peer groups exclusively. So, you could almost say that from there, clinical supervision was adapted for use in the more traditional supervisory setting.

KAREN: I didn't realize that. That makes it all the more understandable why you and Bob [K] seem so adamant about Helping with a capital *H,* as opposed to evaluating with a small *e.*

BOB K: You've got it. Clinical supervision was not intended to be a tool for making judgments and assessments—it was intended as a goal for facilitating growth.

ROOSEVELT: Hey, look at the clock. We'd better get off to our sessions.

BOB A: Yup, time seems to be up. But look, Bob [K] and I are about to send out a questionnaire to forty or fifty people, to get some perceptions about CS directly from the field for our third edition. Could we send it to each of you?
(Nods from the group.)

ROOSEVELT: Send me twenty copies. I'll have all of our department heads fill it out, and then you'll owe me a free copy of the book.

BOB K: You're a tough bargainer! For a start, we'll pick up the check for these refreshments. *(Everyone heads out.)*

A SECOND SCENARIO: THE PRACTITIONERS SPEAK

■ It is three months later. We (the two Bobs) are in Tampa, leafing through the responses to our mailout. The returns have been sorted into piles, one for each role group. We are pleased with the good and often detailed responses that were received.

The questionnaire consisted of seven questions, to each of which an open-ended narrative response was invited. Krajewski has already summarized the material, and offers the following write-up for discussion:

Question 1
In your own experience over the years, how have supervisory services to teachers changed?

Teacher respondents note generally that supervisors:

- are now more accessible to teachers,

- are in and out of the classroom more, and
- have more defined and redefined roles.

Most teachers speak of more teacher involvement in supervision decision making and supervision as a team activity. They perceive observation feedback to be more familiarized (in content and form) and immediate. Several comment on the professional growth plan prepared for them. A sixth-grade Minnesota teacher with 26 years experience is convinced that a principal can make the difference, stating that only in the last two years has she experienced a positive change in supervisory technique. She appreciates that her present principal *trusts* that teachers are professionals, *empowers* teachers with decision making, provides teachers with freedom to experiment and create, and encourages them to take risks and go with what works with kids. One Texas high-school teacher feels that since the advent of the Texas Teacher Appraisal System (TTAS), supervisors have taken on a more adversarial position than ever before, and that the TTAS actually prevents needed support that a more frequent, informal observation system would provide.

Elementary principals corroborate teacher feelings. They think that the supervisor role is:

- more research based on teaching techniques,
- more facilitative,
- more collaborative, and
- more focused on growth.

Supervision, they note, means active involvement. Observation and conferencing *should* occur at least twice each year.

Middle- and high-school principals agree that immediate recent supervision is:

- more formative,
- more goal-oriented, and
- more facilitative and research-based,

thereby providing educators with a sense of professional credibility. A North Carolina respondent comments that in the last six years funding has begun for K–12 administrative positions designated for teacher supervision only, and this has required dialogue and ongoing intervention from supervisors to teachers.

Central office supervision personnel also note more supervisor-teacher involvement, with increased school-level organizational development and collegial counseling. Some relate that classroom supervision is now part of the supervisor's job that is evaluated. Thus training, record keeping and monitoring of supervisory activities have increased significantly. More and more, supervisors are working *with* teachers to create change.

University clinical professor respondents from the southeastern U.S. believe that in the last five years clinical supervision has entered the vocabulary of teachers who serve as cooperating teachers or mentors. Especially to novice teachers, supervisory services have gone from practically none to intensive; mentor training has contributed greatly.

Question 2

If for the moment we may assume that the observer/supervisor is someone whose motives and competence you trust, what kinds of guidance, assistance, and support are you eager to receive, and to what extent do you receive it? How does it benefit you in a growing profession?

Teacher and supervisor responses alike reinforce the assumption that professionals seek support systems encouraging growth and change within an environment of trust. Teacher respondents agree that competent supervisors help them analyze and focus on specific problems or teaching strategies. Most teachers seek *and* appreciate positive feedback and suggestions on weaknesses and strengths through joint problem-solving sessions. For example, a Virginia third-grade teacher, noting that supervisors are recently more accessible to teachers, comments that a conference should be a give-and-take session in a supportive, collegial environment. Teachers recognize a shift in the last few years to a more collegial supervisory relationship with teachers and staff. A Wisconsin teacher with 21 years of experience classifies this revelation as an "open door policy."

Elementary principals commonly agree that the program should enable professional growth and provide frequent, specific feedback. A Texas principal says that she remains contemporary and recognizes growth when she has access to a listening ear and an objective but supportive perspective. A South Carolina assistant principal is eager to receive constructive growth suggestions in any area.

Middle- and high-school principals reflect similar comments regarding significant consequences of supervision. A high-school principal from Florida prefers a more formative support system that encourages risk taking and change. A principal with 23 years of experience, after reflecting on a more autocratic, top-down style of supervision, now admits that principals need to be open, accept criticism, respond to recommendations, and be willing to correct deficiencies.

Central office supervisors note like expectations of evaluation approaches, including collegial coaching programs. From Minnesota, a director of instruction writes that any supervision done in a nonthreatening manner, in an atmosphere of mutual trust and respect, fosters growth. From Ohio, a coordinator feels that by being supportive of teachers, a ground work for other activities and support is in place.

University clinical professors appreciate coaching and supervision on general pedagogy, content-specific pedagogy and moral/ethical reasoning.

They feel that both novice and experienced teachers need to have someone who is supportive, willing to listen to concerns and offer assistance in analyzing teaching effectiveness.

Question 3

How do classroom teachers feel about being supervised? What are some of the specific fears (or other negatives) they have? What benefits do they hope for?

Teachers afforded mixed responses. Most report that supervision in itself produces feelings of anxiety. Anxiety results in a tendency for teachers to resist change, responded a seventh-grade science teacher from Florida who further postulated, "Many teachers like routine. The supervisor is perceived as a critic rather than a colleague who wishes to help." A Minnesota teacher is optimistic that most teachers appreciate open and honest feedback from their principal when an environment of trust exists. A twelfth-grade teacher from Texas concludes that classroom teachers are not afraid of supervision unless the process is connected to career ladder placement, salary increase, or retention issues. A teacher from Wisconsin is receptive to supervisors' suggestions and feels her peers would agree, "Most teachers are looking for better ways to do a difficult job."

Elementary principals recognize that a facilitative atmosphere reduces threat and anxiety towards supervision. A Texas principal comments that teachers hate supervision that causes fear or intimidation. A principal from Minnesota feels his teachers look forward to the supervision model in place there. Teachers want the feedback, the recognition of a job well done, and a furthering of the trust relationship established.

Middle- and high-school principals responded similarly. With the fear of threat reduced, the teacher and supervisor may experience greater communication and cooperation. A North Carolina principal comments that teachers welcome feedback to improve if the supervisor has developed their trust. A Florida principal thinks teachers only fear supervision when it is sporadic and evaluative and based upon what they believe is a one-shot chance. When it is supportive and growth-oriented the fear subsides.

A central office manager from Ohio acknowledges the importance of working with teachers to design and plan change. "Good supervisors," she writes, "work to develop trust and communication with the teachers to create change." From Minnesota, a director of instruction believes that confident and competent teachers like to be supervised by competent and nurturing supervisors.

Clinical professors confirm teachers' nervousness about supervision if coaching and pre- and post-conferencing have not been involved. When assistance and trust are foremost, claims one professor, all teachers seem excited about being supervised as they develop their own supervisory skills.

Question 4

With regard to the people who provide hands-on supervisory services to teachers in the schools, in what area do you think they do best or are the most skilled? In which respects do they need to develop greater skill and expertise?

Teachers concur that supervisors are most skilled at identifying positive aspects of lessons and providing praise for the teacher's skill and effort. Listening skills, collegial support, and providing skill training for teachers also rank high. Several responses indicate that supervisors are stronger in administrative tasks and paperwork obligations. Teachers in general believe supervisors need to be more accessible. From Virginia, a teacher writes that the supervisor's responsibilities need to be limited to enable them to focus on service to teachers. A teacher from Texas suggests that supervisors need to show they have a *personal* interest in the lives of their teachers. From Florida, a teacher feels supervisors need to motivate those around them and recognize their potentials, creating risk-takers who are discontent with the satisfactory evaluations they receive while maintaining their present level of mediocrity.

Elementary principals share a wide range of skills they feel significant to their professional status; however, communication with teachers was not a recurrent area reported. Frequently mentioned are competency in effective school philosophy, knowledge of curriculum and guidance in textbook selection. A Texas supervisor expresses concern at not having the time to observe every teacher; however, others mention encouragement and support to teachers as a skill they have developed.

Desirable competencies recognized by middle- and high-school principals indicate that successful leaders value cooperation, interdependence, and harmonious interaction for success. From North Carolina, a high-school principal comments that effective communication, oral and written, is essential if the supervisor hopes to have a positive impact on teachers. They must be in touch first with the human being, then with the professional. A Minnesota administrator considers involving people in decision making that affects their classrooms an important service to develop. The need for better conferencing, listening, and interpersonal communication skills was expressed as skill areas that need greater development in their middle and high schools. A middle-school principal with 23 years of experience regards motivation of the apathetic student of major concern. Constructing better and more effective assessment procedures was also considered by many. A principal from Florida comments, "We need to develop and employ a cadre of professional teacher trainers to periodically observe and assist teachers at their request."

Central office administrators identify similar strengths and weaknesses in supervisory services to teachers in the schools. A social studies coordinator writes that creation of an atmosphere where change and

growth or risk taking is valued is encouraged in her high school in Ohio. An assistant superintendent of instruction has recently become interested in collegial coaching as a viable supervisory skill.

Clinical professors feel effective mentor training produces skills in listening, problem solving, and assisting persons in self-analyzing teaching performance. Nonetheless, they feel, more training is needed in addressing higher-level teaching skills, learning about research dealing with effective teaching skills and adult development, what coaching involves, how to plan specific strategies that promote growth and development of the individual, and how to conference.

Question 5

In your experience or as you have observed, how much hands-on (clinical) supervision is actually taking place in the school(s)? Should it be more, or less?

In general, teachers comment that clinical supervision is available, particularly, to first year or probationary instructors. A teacher from Florida writes that her school has a good grasp on the process. All administrators are trained in and use the method. In addition, each school in her district has two peer coaches trained in the clinical supervision model. Another instructor with 19 years of experience writes of considerable clinical supervision occurring on a volunteer basis; however, she perceives that those teachers who choose to become involved have achieved a level of expertise already while those who criticize the program should probably be more involved. Fifteen teachers are participating in CS; all have at one time been nominated or elected teacher of the year.

An Oklahoma elementary principal responds that if the administrator is effective, the supervision is at a high level, ongoing and nonthreatening. Therefore, clinical supervision should be continuous. Other elementary principals consider their methods informal, with frequent visits with teachers in their classrooms. "But more," a Minnesota principal says, "needs to be done to develop trust between teachers and administrators."

A Minnesota middle-school principal comments that they have implemented the concept but there should be more; release time for staff is always a problem. From Oklahoma, a high-school principal responds that the boards of education need to support and encourage more of this type of supervision. A mentor program in South Carolina contributes tremendously to heighten teachers' interest in collaborative supervision programs. A principal from Florida reports that over the past four years, a substantial amount of clinical supervision such as peer teachers and collegial coaches, especially for new people, has occurred. There is a need to increase the program for those who consider themselves "experienced"; they tend to be the least accepting.

Central office managers observe more clinical supervision now than ever before. In Florida, teachers are invited to identify areas of concern and are coached, primarily by peers. In Minnesota, a director of instruction writes that every staff member in his district participates in at least one clinical supervision cycle yearly; non-tenured have at least three. He feels this is adequate training. A social studies coordinator, however, notes that the trend is just starting in her school district. She sees the number climbing yearly as the teachers become more interested in this type of supervision. Efforts are made, there, to update principals and assistant principals about clinical supervision.

Clinical professors from North Carolina report that mentors engage in three to five cycles with novice teachers—and feel these should be more available.

Question 6

Professional Interaction: Aside from the interaction that takes place when a supervisor (or coach) and a teacher are working together, how much opportunity do you or your colleagues have to become familiar with each others' work, including problems and successes?

A general consensus among teachers polled is that time is a limiting factor in establishing regular professional interaction opportunities. Clerical responsibilities and classload diminish the opportunity. In one Texas high school, teachers have little chance for interaction. It takes a constant concerted effort on the part of colleagues to work together and keep in touch; however, one respondent feels the teachers and, therefore, the students could benefit greatly with more sharing/cooperating time. Some teachers, such as one from Texas, utilize the lunch hours to share ideas. A teacher from Virginia agrees that time is the greatest enemy, but feels the experience of sharing is a vital part of the building of trust and collegial respect. A Wisconsin teacher writes that they have daily team meetings which provide an excellent opportunity to share successes and concerns. Teachers there often team for projects. A teacher in Florida discovered her involvement in the Collegial Coach program in her district offers increased occasions for sharing successes and discussing shortcomings. As professionals, she writes, we need to shake the fear that someone may find out we are not perfect.

Elementary principals offer similar reactions. They, too, are frustrated with the lack of time and opportunity for professional interaction with peers. A principal from South Carolina responds that there is not nearly enough opportunity to become familiar with successes. There always seems to be too much time devoted to problems.

A Wisconsin middle-school principal encourages this type of engagement at staff meetings, workshops, and inservices to help teachers become familiar with one another's jobs. He sees peer interaction as limited but improving each year.

Clinical professors report a continuum of opportunity, from minimal to frequent interaction. The high school interaction, one claims, depends on the principal's receptivity to faculty meeting to share ideas and on the department chair's level of encouragement to faculty.

Question 7
If the educational world were perfect, what kind of a supervisory program would there be?

From the teachers' point of view, identification of the ideal supervisory system means solutions of issues that affect their professional world. Some feel it would be beneficial for teachers to assume a part in the managerial functions associated with teaching and share in planning, organizing, and controlling services. From Florida, a seventh-grade teacher suggests that all teachers have the opportunity to alternately participate as coach and peer; administrators would serve as facilitators. A Texas fifth-grade teacher envisions similar changes; master teachers would be used in a supervisory capacity, mentoring teachers who need more direct supervision with formal time allocated for interaction and planning. A teacher from Virginia suggests that supervisors could play a valuable role in keeping teachers knowledgeable of current research, providing resources and ideas.

Elementary principals would erase the illusory demarcation line impeding collaborative efforts between teachers and supervisors. From Ohio, a principal describes the concept of a team of people working *together* at all levels. A principal from Oklahoma idealizes that if perfection were achievable, all staff would function at total effectiveness and supervision would be minimal, if any. In an ideal school system in South Carolina, the principal would encourage a daily flow of many expert supervisors in classrooms. Ideas would be exchanged in a non-threatening, safe environment where the students would be of the utmost importance.

Time and budget constraints are a limiting factor for middle- and high-school principals in achieving their ideal goals. In Florida, a middle-school principal would like to see a team of professional teacher trainers whose sole responsibility would be to work with teachers to improve instruction by being supportive, providing information, demonstrating effective techniques, and being available to administrators to assist both veteran and beginning teachers. A high-school principal from North Carolina responds that the ideal supervisory program would be one that offers ongoing training for teachers and administrators, has university consultants available for advice, and involves trained teachers in facilitating roles. A principal from Wisconsin also mentions peer observation as a component of an ideal system.

In Minnesota, a director of instruction idealizes a system where everyone helps each other to be more successful. Fear would be eliminated as mistakes and improvements are made. A director from Ohio suggests each

teacher would design an improvement plan and work alongside a supervisor; growth and encouragement would be fostered by both.

In North Carolina, a clinical professor offers professional development centers as one avenue. Developing a cadre of on-site teacher educators at every school offers broader possibilities: long-term training for teacher educators, ongoing support and assistance, realistic placement for novice teachers, reduced teaching levels for supervising teachers and colleagues, school- and district-wide support for coaching and supervision, and collaborative arrangements between local education agencies (LEAs) and institutions of higher education (IHEs). Other suggestions included on-site trained mentors to work with both novice and experienced teachers, flexible scheduling for mentors, and time to provide coaching.

SUMMARY

Bob A: These responses confirm that quite a shift has been taking place in professionals' attitudes toward supervision.

Bob K: You see it as a shift in the right direction?

Bob A: Indeed, yes! Not so many years ago, when I polled the teachers in my graduate classes in supervision, the typical response to Question 3 [how teachers feel about CS] would have been much more anxiety-oriented.

Bob K: And probably you'd have had shorter answers to Question 5 [how much CS is occurring].

Bob A: By shorter you probably mean they would have reported that little, if any, CS was going on. That's very true. I remember one class in 1985 where out of twenty-nine teachers in the room, only three remembered a classroom observation during the past twelve months that was for other than some administrative/evaluative purpose. Several even reported their principals filled out their annual teacher evaluation checksheet without coming into the classroom at all.

Bob K: Maybe that still goes on, but from these responses I perceive that we're making progress.

Bob A: I was intrigued by the frequent reference to collegiality, and to peer supervision or mentoring as a valued aspect of the adult school experience.

Bob K: Well, during the last five years or so there has been more literature on the need for teachers to work and share together than perhaps in the previous half-century.

Bob A: And hooray for that. Happily, this coincides with welcome noise about the changing role of the principal—

BOB K: —as the head coach of the instructional team?

BOB A: Why not? The term *coaching* has become much more respectable in the last few years.

BOB K: More popular than the term *evaluating*, that's for sure.

BOB A: I was interested in what that Florida principal said about the difference between one-shot, sporadic supervision as opposed to continuous, supportive, and growth-oriented supervision.

BOB K: In a sense, that remark symbolizes where, hopefully, we are heading.

BOB A: And so, I think, do the numerous references to trust... or implicitly to one of your favorite words, *rapport*.

BOB K: If you don't have it, you're in trouble.

BOB A: Well, now you're jumping ahead to Chapter 4.

BOB K: Perhaps. But first we need to take all of this material on the table, this "reality" stuff that has come from people out there in the field at both ends of the CS relationship, and see how it fits into our thinking about the qualities of an effective supervisor.

(The scene fades. Screen credits and sincere thanks to the good people from Florida, Ohio, Texas, Oklahoma, Minnesota, South Carolina, Virginia, Wisconsin, and North Carolina whose thoughtful questionnaire responses enriched this discussion.)

REFERENCES

[1] Morris Cogan, *Clinical Supervision*, Houghton Mifflin, Boston, 1973, p. 9.

[2] Thomas J. Sergiovanni and Robert J. Starratt, *Supervision: Human Perspectives*, 4th ed., McGraw-Hill, New York, 1988, p. 304.

[3] Keith A. Acheson and Meredith Damien Gall, *Techniques in the Clinical Supervision of Teachers: Preservice and Inservice Applications*, 2nd ed., Longman, New York, 1987, pp.1 and 11.

[4] Ned A. Flanders, "Interaction Analysis and Clinical Supervision," *Journal of Research and Development in Education 9*, Winter 1976, pp. 47–48.

[5] John Lovell and Kimball Wiles, *Supervision for Better Schools*, 5th ed., Prentice-Hall, Englewood Cliffs, N.J., 1983, p. 69.

[6] Karolyn J. Snyder, "Clinical Supervision," in *Encyclopedia of School Administration and Supervision*, ed. by Richard Gorton, Oryx Press, Phoenix, 1988, p. 261.

[7] John C. Daresh, *Supervision as a Proactive Process*, Longman, New York, 1989, p. 218.

[8] Don M. Beach and Judy Reinhartz, *Supervision: Focus on Instruction*, Harper and Row, New York, 1989, p. 156.

[9] Peter F. Oliva, *Supervision for Today's Schools*, 3rd ed., Longman, New York, 1989, p. 503.

[10] Carl Glickman, *Supervision of Instruction: A Developmental Approach*, 2nd ed., Allyn & Bacon, Boston, 1990, pp. 280–307.

CHAPTER

2

SUPERVISOR ROLE RESPONSIBILITIES

In This Chapter

- Supervision as a Dimension of Leadership
- Qualities for Successful Business Leadership
- Qualities for Successful Medical Leadership
- Qualities for Successful Supervisor Leadership
- Instructional Supervision
- Clinical Supervision
- Implications for the Effective Supervisor
- Summary

CLINICAL SUPERVISION

CONTENTS

Editor-in-Chief Ted Buchholz
Acquisitions Editor Jo-Anne Weaver
Senior Project Editor Cliff Crouch
Production Manager Jane Tyndall Ponceti
Book Designers Carol Kincaid, Peggy Young
Electronic Publishing Supervisor Michael Beaupré
Electronic Publishing Coordinator Jill Stubblefield

Library of Congress Catalog Card Number: 92-153793
ISBN: 0-03-073143-7

Address editorial correspondence to: 301 Commerce Street, Suite 3700
Fort Worth, Texas 76102
Address orders to: 6277 Sea Harbor Drive
Orlando, Florida 32887
1-800-782-4479, or 1-800-433-0001 (in Florida)

Printed in the United States of America

2 3 4 5 6 7 8 9 0 1 2 039 9 8 7 6 5 4 3 2 1

CLINICAL SUPERVISION
SPECIAL METHODS FOR THE SUPERVISION OF TEACHERS

THIRD EDITION

ROBERT GOLDHAMMER

LATE OF THE UNIVERSITY OF PITTSBURGH

ROBERT H. ANDERSON

UNIVERSITY OF SOUTHERN FLORIDA

ROBERT J. KRAJEWSKI

UNIVERSITY OF WISCONSIN—LA CROSSE

HARCOURT BRACE JOVANOVICH COLLEGE PUBLISHERS

Fort Worth Philadelphia San Diego New York Orlando Austin San Antonio
Toronto Montreal London Sydney Tokyo

What does the term *supervision* imply? What activities comprise it? In 1931, the Department of Supervisors and Directors of Instruction of the National Education Association answered these questions in this way:

> All activities by which educational officers may express leadership in the improvement of teaching. Such activities as observation of classroom instruction, conduct of teachers' meetings and of group and individual conferences are clearly within the meaning of this term. The development and execution of plans looking toward increased effectiveness in reading, arithmetic, and some other area of the school program, and the organization or reorganization of curriculum and method are still further examples of what is meant by supervisory activities.[1]

In the decades since, many scholars of supervision have offered their views. Some perceive supervision as checking on compliance with prescribed teaching techniques, or the production of new courses of study and curricula. Others see it largely as being concerned with managerial responsibilities outside of the fields of curriculum and instruction. Still others see it as working with professional personnel to seek new answers or to release potential energies of teachers who wish to find answers for themselves.

Many other possibilities come to mind. In the absence of a precise definition it is possible for educators, whether they supervise or are supervised, to be influenced by the personal values, political orientations, and educational philosophies that operate in the background. In turn, the varied perceptions cause individuals to elect certain activities and accept certain responsibilities while rejecting other possibilities.

It would be a challenging endeavor to define what constitutes effective supervision in the 1990s. Of course, a definition by itself does not reveal the complexities of the supervisory leadership role. It may be useful to provide at this point a brief overview of supervision as a dimension of leadership, including examples of effective leadership qualities from the medical and business fields, and then examine at least briefly the role that instructional and clinical supervision play, or could play, within leadership for more effective teaching.

SUPERVISION AS A DIMENSION OF LEADERSHIP

■ Often linked with educational administration, and invariably connected with the concept of educational leadership, *supervision is today seen as that dimension of the teaching profession which is concerned with improving instructional effectiveness.* Nearly all definitions of supervision include components such as stimulating staff growth and development, influencing teacher behaviors in the classroom or counseling center, and fostering the selection, development, integral use, and evaluation of good instructional approaches and materials. Some definitions particularly stress the role of communication skills in supervision, and in recent years a strong emphasis has developed on helping teachers with problem-solving, with interpersonal relationships within the school, and with creating a more humane atmosphere to surround children and the adults who teach them.

Nearly all discussions of supervision in textbooks and periodicals have wrestled with the difficult problem of separating *helping* behaviors from *evaluating* behaviors on the part of supervisors, since the helping functions have most often been assigned to the same persons (principals, department heads, directors) who are at times responsible for decisions about employment, promotions, salary matters, or all three functions. Compounding this problem is that, especially since the 1983 publication of *A Nation at Risk* and the ensuing wave of legislation aimed at removing or disciplining nonperforming teachers through rigorous appraisal/evaluation systems, there is in many schools an atmosphere of mistrust in the competency of the teacher corps.[2]

It is regrettable that this apparent lack of public confidence in teacher competency, as seen in the legislative mandates that stem from it, has contaminated the supervisory situation in many schools. Anderson (op. cit.)[3] has called for a "presumption of competency," parallel to the U.S. legal system's presumption of an accused person's innocence until guilt is proven.

A small number of teachers are incompetent, and no one would argue that, following due process, they should be removed from the schools. Some teachers also currently perform at a level below the standard, but can be brought to a higher, more adequate level through skillful supervisory and collegial assistance. For this latter group, CS can be of great benefit. It seems to us, however, that the great majority of teachers are both hardworking and reasonably competent; and these persons, too, deserve the benefit of empathetic, positively oriented CS. Even superstars can profit from CS, as we will argue repeatedly in this volume. Were school leaders to function in obvious ways on the assumption that teachers are competent unless proved otherwise, a healthier atmosphere would exist and teachers would be far more likely to perceive supervision as a friendly and welcome activity, rather than a threat.

The dimension of administrative work that includes assessing, evaluating, and judging should be considered as separate from those *supportive* functions for which supervision (as contrasted with administration) is the appropriate label: coaching, helping, and facilitating growth. Supportive supervision will also involve invigoration of the organization itself, contributing to the accomplishment of district and individual *stretch goals*, assisting groups in realizing their missions effectively, fostering self-evaluation by both individuals and groups, and nurturing a healthy work culture.

We propose that those charged with both the helping, as we have defined it, and the evaluating functions seek to regard CS as one of the most powerful tools in their *helping* repertory and to regard the contents of this book, as indeed the contents of all supervision volumes, as concerned almost exclusively with that dimension of their work. Our intent is primarily to serve the interests of those whose single-minded interest is in helping professional workers to thrive.

The following table summarizes essential characteristics of supervision, broadly defined, during seven periods of educational history.

TABLE 1

COMPARISON OF PERIODS OF SUPERVISION, EARLY 1900S TO PRESENT

1850–1920	Scientific Management
1920–1930	Democratic Interaction Approach
1930–1955	Cooperative Supervision
1955–1965	Supervision as Curriculum Development
1965–1970	Impact of Clinical Supervision Ideas
1970–1985	Group Dynamics/Peer Emphasis
1985–1990s	Coaching/Instructional Supervision

As the table illustrates, supervision has progressed, at least at the theoretical level, through overlapping periods, each of which had certain dominant features. Early on, supervisors tended to fulfill their roles by inspecting for compliance with ordered teaching techniques. Lucio and McNeil have pointed out that through the first quarter of the twentieth century, "teachers were regarded as instruments that should be closely supervised to insure that they mechanically carried out the methods of procedure determined by administrative and special supervisors."[4] It might be acknowledged that given the meager training possessed by most teachers up to World War II or so, and also given the very limited conceptual framework undergirding public education, the inspectorial approach probably could be defended.

As understandings of child growth and development matured, and education became a more sophisticated field of study, teachers functioned within a different framework, and their needs for supervision changed. During several successive eras, the focus of supervision was on helping teachers to develop as thoughtful instructors and to be more aware of, and skillful in, interactive and cooperative approaches. The role of the supervisor was gradually shifting to that of a colleague, albeit superordinate to some extent; and as schools became more concerned with the need for significant curriculum development, the supervisor's role shifted from that of enforcer to that of co-builder. Especially after the Soviets launched the world's first man-made satellite, *Sputnik I,* in 1957, a national frenzy of curriculum innovation caused the supervisor to become more involved in not only the promulgation of new programs but also the attendant staff-development activities as well. Supervision as a dimension of leadership was beginning to gain acceptance.

With the emergence of CS in the late 1960s came another major shift in the role played by supervisors. Although the literature of clinical supervision did not emerge as a strong force until the 1970s, the late 1960s saw a sharp increase in interest in direct intervention technologies. Stimulated in part by the development of team teaching and other collegial arrangements, teachers began to interact with one another more frequently and intensely, and supervisors were called upon more often to assist in analyzing current classroom practice, the operant curriculum, and person-to-person relationships.

One effect of these developments was an increase of interest in classroom observations and conferencing as a means for improving programs and teaching. These authors, looking through the supervision textbooks published before the mid-1970s, have been struck by their paucity (and in some cases total absence) of commentary about how to use classroom visits as a supervisory tool. Since the classroom visit before this time was almost always related to the making of administrative judgments, perhaps this gap in the literature should not surprise us. However, for the past 20 or so years, classroom visits and observations as a legitimate part of staff development (and program development) have gained almost universal acceptance, and every supervision textbook deals with the topic in some detail. Often, the discussion includes, or falls within, material about the clinical supervision cycle.

The survey reported in Chapter 1, along with the materials in other supervision writings, provides evidence of a shift, which continues in the 1990s, from formal and authoritarian supervisory methods to a more informal, interactive, and client-friendly approach. *It is now much clearer that the major purpose of supervision is leadership improvement of instruction and of the instructional environment, geared to carefully defined and cooperatively developed goals.* The shift in these directions has its natural roots in the emphases upon cooperative group work and democratic human relations in the 1930s, '40s, and '50s. Supervision today is clearly seen as an integral dimension of leadership.

Now let us examine the qualities of effective leadership in two related fields to better determine the leadership influence in educational supervision.

QUALITIES FOR SUCCESSFUL BUSINESS LEADERSHIP

■ In recent years, educators have become increasingly familiar with the literature of leadership in fields other than education. As a matter of fact, ideas about how to manage corporations, factories, military units, governmental agencies, medical institutions, and other production-oriented organizations have permeated educational units for at least a hundred years. One could reasonably argue that nearly all of the historically dominant theories about educational leadership and school management had their origins in the world of work. This has had both positive and negative effects upon pupils and school employees, with the negatives (notably, as reflected in what Callahan labelled "the cult of efficiency") seeming to prevail.

In the last ten or fifteen years, however, two welcome things have happened. The first is that scholars and practitioners in the world of work have been constructing new leadership paradigms based upon what seem to be more humane and enlightened views of productivity in the workplace. Evidence of the shift in this direction may be found in the burgeoning (almost explosive) literature in which Tom Peters, Robert Waterman, John Naisbitt, Rosabeth Moss Kanter, Peter Drucker, Alvin Toffler, Ralph Kilmann, Richard Boyatzis, and others have defined leadership as primarily a function of human resource development, and have proposed that organizations must in effect turn themselves upside-down and inside-out if their members are to become as creative and productive as possible.

These authors claim that, as never before, the frontline employee (or the classroom teacher in our frame of reference) must be as close to goal-setting and decision-making as possible, and problem-solving and entrepreneurial adventuring must be the special focus of organizational life. The "work culture" of the organization must be one in which shared visions, strong sense of commitment to well-defined goals, lively communication, high levels of trust, goal-oriented risk-taking, and continuous growth and learning are omnipresent. In such a context, the functions of supervision take on a very special, positive, supportive dimension.

It may be appropriate, therefore, to take a few moments to reflect upon definitions of leadership as they appear in such literature. A conversation with Ronald Bottin (dean of the business school at Southwest Missouri State University) and David Glass (chief executive officer of Wal-Mart) helped us in formulating this section.

For a majority of business and professional people, success is proportional to the ability to be a leader. The portrait of a leader is one who helps an organization establish a shared vision of a common goal, thereby performing as a manager of the goal-achievement process. Leadership, in its basic form, is not a function of age or position; anyone in any position can lead at any time. Leadership is simply the art of enabling and/or persuading people to go along with a certain idea.

However, leaders must go beyond simply accomplishing tasks. They must also provide direction and organization for the group. Successful direction and organization require a great amount of convincing, requesting, directing, and coordinating. Most importantly, though, successful leaders provide participative leadership, which is dependent upon solid communication between and among subordinates and their leaders.

Along with the above characteristics, leaders must realize that in many ways they set the tone of the organization. If the leader is hard-driving, the culture of the company will tend to be so, too. If the leader is a risk-taker, the company will tend to be adventurous and innovative. It is important here to differentiate between the tone that the leader sets and the ego of the leader. A leader must never let his or her ego get in the way of the organization's best interest.

While the best leaders seem to possess a certain knack to lead, anyone can become a better leader. To further the skills of both present and future leaders, several key areas should be addressed. Those who command the respect, loyalty, and willing efforts of others normally have eight qualities in common:

1. **Vision leading to a sense of mission.**
   Vision sets leaders apart. The difference between a manager and a leader is focus and vision.

2. **Communication of this mission in a way that inspires confidence and contribution.**
   Good leaders express their mission in more than words and in ways that make the vision seem attainable. "Managers manage things, where leaders not only lead but inspire people."

3. **The ability to lead rather than dictate.**
   Good leaders use participatory leadership to enable the hierarchies of power to flatten out. They are diplomatic and democratic. They use macromanagement rather than micromanagement styles.

4. **The courage to promote innovation and encourage risks.**
   Effective leaders convey the message that innovation is important by leading the charge personally. They encourage experimentation. They take chances and readily accept error. "Fear of failure must never be a reason not to try something different."

5. **Dedication and persistence.**
   Successful corporate leaders do their homework and develop expertise. Strength and flexibility are key elements for entrepreneurial accomplishment. As setbacks occur, good leaders bounce back.

6. **Emotional balance.**
   Good leaders do what they believe is right, even at the risk of being disliked. They develop enthusiasm for the matter at hand. They use humor whenever possible to create a friendly atmosphere.

7. **Care for excellence and people.**
   The key to making a high-commitment organization is mutual trust between top executives and employees. Fairness and equity ultimately lead to genuine concern for employees. Good leaders pay strict attention to quality and details.

8. **The ability to simplify.**
   Good leaders strive for refined, simple answers to complex questions. They focus on essentials. They streamline the actions of functional areas to avoid excessive efforts.

Perhaps the decisive quality of a leader has been best described by Franklin D. Roosevelt: "The final test of a leader is that he leaves behind him in other men the conviction and the will to carry on."

QUALITIES FOR SUCCESSFUL MEDICAL LEADERSHIP

■ From the beginning, those involved in clinical supervision development knew that the word *clinical* evoked some negative images—supervisory "treatment" or "providing cures" by placement in a medical clinic. Robert Goldhammer tried to convey (as we also do now) the image of face-to-face relationships between supervisors and teachers, close observation, detailed observational data, and an intensity of focus that links supervisors and teachers together in an intimate professional relationship.

To help the reader better understand what goes on in a medical clinic, we present the following example.

In La Crosse, Wisconsin, stands the Gunderson Clinic and Lutheran Hospital, a complete medical center with 3,600 employees. Established in 1899, the center in 1989 had more than 550,000 patient clinic visits (2,500 per day) and more than 17,000 hospital admissions and 95,000 patient days. The clinic's education and research division was established in 1944. It now sponsors various residency programs (three years for internal medicine; five years for surgery; three months for residents affiliated with the

Mayo Clinic or the state universities of Iowa, of Minnesota, or of Wisconsin; 15 to 20 students at fourth year; a one-year transitional program, and so forth). There are approximately 60 residents a day, with new ones coming continually. All are medical school graduates.

A consistent and tremendous commitment to graduate education exists at this clinic. The library, containing 20,000 volumes of health-sciences texts and journals, is available to residents 24 hours a day through their own personal keys. The graduate program is accredited and must be evaluated every three years. The clinic is a true academic atmosphere with a strong emphasis on practical experiences.

The cornerstone of the teaching program is the more than 260-physician clinic staff who also serve as faculty (the majority of whom have teaching appointments at university medical schools). All are active practitioners, and many are involved in clinical research. Research programs, conducted by staff with assistance from residents, include areas such as reading disabilities, speech pathology, and surgical management of patients.

Faculty and residents learn together in a symbiotic relationship. Twice each day—at 8 AM and noon—residents and staff gather for medical teaching conferences. Included each week are at least two nationally recognized visiting consultants. "When I have a resident with me," noted Thomas Lathrop, a staff physician, "it forces me to stay current. If one asks a question I cannot answer, you better believe it sends me to the library. This makes me a better physician. The bottom line is that the patients get better care." The respect staff and residents have for one another provides a stimulating, comfortable learning environment for all. Staff provides help when needed; other than that, the residents are given a fair amount of latitude. The result is excellent patient care. The prevailing philosophy of the program is expressed in the title of an expository videotape, *Where the Art of Medicine Becomes Reality.* With an approachable staff and excellent residents, everyone can proceed with new ideas and learn from patients.

Dr. Edwin Overholt, Internist and Foundation/Clinic Director of Medical Education, states, "Our graduate education program has provided the springboard to attract an outstanding staff. On a daily basis, it also puts pressure on the staff in the institution to upgrade the quality of care. *We teach because we believe it is the best way to learn.*"

In an interview, Dr. Overholt presented to us his ideas on what qualities make for successful medical leadership:

1. Possessing a broad base of expertise, and the willingness to grow and seek self-education; being zealous for new knowledge to better resolve the challenges faced each day.

2. Serving as an active role model; being willing to get out in front of the pack in reaching for latest approaches through research.

3. Looking at supervision enthusiastically as an opportunity to provide leadership.
4. Being impeccably honest, providing trust and communication through dialogue, being a good listener, and recognizing that not all good thoughts and ideas are yours.
5. Possessing strong self-discipline and setting mission priorities to provide direction to move forward and do a better job.
6. Being respectful, not denigrating; being accessible, not aloof; being positive and enjoying your opportunities; extending yourself to assist colleagues in times of need; offering understanding when possible.
7. Maintaining an appropriate balance between work and outside interests.

This unique medical clinic may be likened to an ideal school where learning and training occur simultaneously. It is perhaps closest to the type of school envisioned by Cogan, Anderson, and Goldhammer in their early work with the Harvard clinical supervision model.

QUALITIES FOR SUCCESSFUL SUPERVISOR LEADERSHIP

■ From these examples in business and medicine we see the growing awareness that leadership is "situational"; that both the work context and the relative skill and maturity of the workers will be specific to each unique situation, and therefore the leader's activities and approaches should fit the situation as closely as possible. While work contexts may differ, certain leadership principles are universal and should be adapted to client needs. Paul Hersey and Kenneth Blanchard, scholars of business management, are credited with stimulating current interest in this way of thinking and in providing useful models. As scholars of leadership develop theories and explanations, it becomes ever more apparent that leaders over the centuries, even in primitive societies, have had to take individual and situational differences into account.

Since supervision is inherently a leadership function, we think it reasonable to draw from the broadest of leadership literature as we describe the personal and professional make-up of an effective supervisor. We also think it appropriate to draw upon the ever-expanding literature on the qualities, skills, and practices of effective teachers. That literature is at least as subjective as the leadership literature, and is heavily weighted in the direction of philosophical and ethical considerations. It builds upon centuries-old notions about the child as a precious societal resource and the teacher as a potential shaper of the world through his or her influence on the minds and spirits of its future citizens.

In recent years views of the teacher have shifted—from the teacher as a dispenser of knowledge to the teacher as a facilitator of learning. Teaching is increasingly defined as guiding the young into self-directed inquiry and exploration, whereas not so long ago instructional events were more teacher-directed and the child occupied a more passive, subservient role. While such distinctions may be oversimplified, top-down classroom management is now less valued than enabling management.

We assume that nearly all our readers have had ample exposure to current thought about broad trends in leadership and teaching, so that no further elaboration of this point is needed. We will, however, examine one summary statement about the qualities of successful teachers. Duke proposes that successful teachers are characterized by:

1. The ability to diagnose student learning.
2. The selection of appropriate learning procedures.
3. Clear communication of expectations.
4. Maintenance of an orderly learning environment.
5. Continuous monitoring of student progress.
6. Caring for students (respect, acceptance, support and recognition)[5]

Duke's is a good list, although we are inclined to add:

7. Promotion of a participative, interactive human environment.

This last item may be implicit in some of the others, but in light of the increasing attention being paid to pupil learning groups, pupil peer-coaching, tutoring, and other forms of pupil-to-pupil interaction for learning purposes, it merits special mention.

So now let us take this expanded list of seven things a successful teacher does well and see how it pertains to supervisors. As supervisors work with teachers either singly or in groups, proficiency in these seven areas will be attended to continually. Helping teachers to become better diagnosticians of pupil progress and needs, more successful architects of learning situations, more skillful communicators of expectations, better environmental managers, expert monitors, more caring custodians and nurturers of children, and more effective managers of meaningful group experiences, is an excellent and productive role for the supervisor.

The supervisor, too, is a teacher. Teachers learn their profession in a never-ending cycle. Not a day goes by in the life of a teacher, however expert or experienced, without confronting something new or different. There is therefore never a day when something cannot be added to one's reservoir of knowledge or repertory of pedagogical behavior. This being the case, there is probably never a day in which even super-teachers could not benefit from or be reinforced by interaction with a skilled supervisor.

What sorts of talents and skills should the effective supervisor therefore possess? In this volume are many answers to this question. As a start,

Duke's list (expanded to seven items) may again be relevant. As one who is in a sense a teacher of adults, the successful supervisor should be able to:

1. Diagnose the (differential) needs and potential of each teacher for whom he or she is responsible, and thus develop an understanding of each one's current skills and knowledge base.
2. Select the supervisory approach appropriate to each teacher, drawing upon this understanding.
3. Communicate effectively with each teacher, especially about potential areas of growth and improvement.
4. Maintain a comfortable yet businesslike relationship with the teacher, focused on continuous professional learning.
5. Stay in touch with each teacher's progress toward well-defined improvement goals.
6. Demonstrate a supportive, respectful, and caring relationship with each teacher.
7. Help teachers to make meaningful and productive connections with one another, and support and facilitate the functioning of all working groups (e.g., teams, task forces, committees, peer-coaching partnerships).

INSTRUCTIONAL SUPERVISION

■ Sometimes the supervisor's role is too broadly defined, and it varies from school system to school system as to responsibilities and title. The supervisor may be referred to as a *helping teacher, lead teacher, instructional specialist, master teacher, coordinator, curriculum specialist, educational assistant, consultant, advisor, instructional assistant, assistant superintendent (for curriculum or instruction), department head, director,* and the like.

The Dictionary of Education defines supervision as:

> all efforts of designated school officials directed toward providing leadership to teachers and other educational workers in the improvement of instruction; involves the stimulation of professional growth and development of teachers, the selection and revision of education objectives, materials of instruction, and methods of teaching, and the evaluation of instruction.[6]

We define supervision as *those activities that improve the quality of teaching and stimulate professional growth and the attainment of "stretch goals" of all participants, thereby nurturing a healthy, invigorating and effective work culture.* Thus, we support and agree with the definition provided by the *Dictionary of Education* except for its emphasis on evaluation of instruction. In our view, such functions as coaching, helping, and facilitating professional growth should dominate a legitimate definition of supervision; work which includes assessing, evaluating, and judging deserves much less visibility within descriptions of the supervisory role.

Most current scholars and significant practitioners would probably agree that when we use the term *instructional supervision* we embrace *those activities engaged in by school personnel specifically to improve the instructional program through influencing or changing teacher behaviors.* Implicit in this definition is that *the instructional dimension of supervision is both a concept and a process aimed at improving and increasing pupil learning.* Lovell and Wiles appear to agree, stating that instructional supervision is a formal organizational activity "for the purpose of interacting with the teaching behavior system in such a way as to maintain, change, and improve the design and actualization of learning opportunities for students."[7]

We see instructional supervision as a subset of general supervision; the latter incorporates all efforts, while instructional supervision is more focused. Yet, the role of the instructional supervisor, though more refined today than in the past, lacks the precision and consistency it deserves in both intra- and inter-school district applications.

Why? One major reason is the inconsistency in job titles and job descriptions for supervisors. Seldom is there one person or agency within a school system solely responsible for providing instructional supervision. Rather—sometimes because of budgetary constraints or even the lower priority assigned to improvement of teaching—such responsibilities are assigned to whichever persons or departments seem best able to absorb them without much disturbance to the other, survival-oriented, work that must be done.

In the 1988 yearbook of the National Society for the Study of Education, *Critical Issues in Curriculum*, several problems and questions related to curriculum are addressed in depth. These include the impact of the constant ebb and flow in curriculum fads, fashions, and rituals upon people in the schools; difficulties in the application of new knowledge; struggles for control over curriculum policy and related program-implementation activities; uneven progress in dealing with program changes and redefined leadership roles; and problems in dealing with the never-ending political pressures felt by supervisors and other school leaders in their struggle to move the instructional program forward in good directions.

In one chapter dealing with the topic of political pressures, Anderson notes that energy for instructional leadership is often diverted into essentially administrative work that helps the school board and superintendent's office cope with the constant pressure from interest groups and other forces. For example, "fire-fighting" assignments (such as gathering data to keep a group or a state agency at bay) often thwart regular assignments. Being (or at least feeling) beleaguered, school districts do not hesitate to postpone or even cancel that work. When this posture persists over a period of years, the result for program updating and teacher revitalization can be disastrous.[8]

In some school systems, therefore, the status and the roles of instructional supervisors remain varied and ambiguous. Where the time and energy of such persons is appropriately protected, a dynamic and supportive program of leadership can be provided. Where resources are not protected or made available, however, the people at the school-building level may be forced to depend largely on their own efforts and resources.

Unfortunately, principals are often as beleaguered and time-pressured as their central office colleagues; and while it is increasingly fashionable to talk about the instructional-leadership role of the principal, often that person is hard pressed to do the job well. Andrews and Soder note that it is unrealistic to expect principals to extend their responsibilities to include significant attention to instructional supervisory functions:

> Realistically the "day-to-day" needs of the school are so demanding there simply are not enough hours in the day for instructional leadership activities. They are expected to be instructional leaders but the school districts reward them for well-managed, efficiently operated schools.[9]

It is tempting to become pessimistic about the chances for adequate instructional supervision. Yet embedded in most of the legislation and related state mandates for school restructuring and revitalization are provisions for significant attention to program changes, staff development, and the enhancement of pupil learning. We perceive growing awareness at top levels of state government and in local districts of the need to provide resources to protect these functions. It is our hope that instructional supervision will, in the years ahead, grow in size and importance, and that the increased use of CS will reinforce and augment that trend.

CLINICAL SUPERVISION

■ Most of the terminology now commonly associated with clinical supervision derives from, and extends, the model developed at Harvard University by Morris Cogan and his colleagues, and from the work and writings of that group. Psychological "ownership" of the concepts and processes of CS is fortunately now widespread; furthermore, the literature has been enriched by so many and in so many ways that an orthodoxy cannot (and should not) be claimed. CS is thus a dynamic leadership phenomenon whose shape cannot be perfectly described and whose features, virtues, and limitations are viewed in many ways. All the same, the authors do indeed settle upon and elect to identify and advocate certain features which for them have validity.

Of the authors of this volume, Robert Goldhammer was a graduate student of both Robert Anderson and Morris Cogan, and Anderson was a colleague of Cogan during the years that the term *clinical supervision* was adopted by Cogan and that CS was developed as a helping model. In a summer training program managed by Harvard in two schools in Lexington, Massachusetts, from 1960 through 1964, the five-stage observation cycle was a major training component; and Goldhammer, a faculty member in that program, under Anderson's direction drew upon his experience with the cycle for his doctoral dissertation and later for his 1969 book (of which this volume is the third edition). Cogan, who finished his distinguished career at the University of Pittsburgh, brought Goldhammer and others from the Harvard group into his faculty, and in 1973 his own book on the same topic added depth and dimension to the subject. This volume, then, derives from the Harvard experience and its several offshoots. That others have built other models and offered somewhat different descriptions is seen as highly desirable.

As noted in the opening chapter, CS definitions include such elements as "up-close," "improvement of teaching performance," "objective observation and analysis of teaching," "face-to-face," and "collegial practice." Our own definition is quite consistent with all these, and in a sense enhances the common elements. CS, as we see it, is *that aspect of supervision which draws upon data from first-hand observation of actual teaching, or other professional events, and involves face-to-face and other associated interactions between the observer(s) and person(s) observed in the course of analyzing the observed professional behaviors and activities and seeking to define and/or develop next steps toward improved performance.*

Implicit in this definition is that CS can involve different facilitators and beneficiaries. By "observer(s)" we mean those persons attempting to help; and by "person(s) being observed" we refer to all sorts of persons being helped: teachers, counselors, principals, supervisors, directors, and so on.

Over the years, and with new editions of this volume, the authors' own views of CS and our definition of it have changed in one particular respect: now, more than ever, we stress the dimension of *collegiality*, and urge that CS be seen as a tool for use in not only the usual superordinate-subordinate relationship but also peer relationships as well. Professional self-containment is no longer acceptable or fruitful, and teachers can enjoy much more productive lives within collegial settings (such as team teaching provides).

We perceive that the clinical dimension of supervision is more clearly defined and causes less confusion than *instructional supervision* and the larger, all-inclusive *general supervision*. Because CS is more focused and specific, and stimulates and depends upon a greater amount of participation and interaction, it is probably easier for the involved parties to understand, accept, and function within their respective roles. Also, because the teacher (or other "helpee") is a direct client and has a direct stake in both the focus and the outcome of the CS process, the process will likely be welcomed. Less likely, by contrast, is an enthusiastic and appreciative response to instructional supervision activities aimed more broadly at groups of teachers. CS tends to be very personal, and it also tends to be fruitful.

IMPLICATIONS FOR THE EFFECTIVE SUPERVISOR

■ One can infer that describing the role of the supervisor and instructional supervisor is a difficult task. Yet the question of the role description for the instructional supervisor remains unanswered and demands immediate attention. Ideally, this description should be arrived at by instructional supervisors and their clients, and then be understood, agreed upon, and used by all concerned. Its delineation should be available for reading by all professional personnel in the school system. Once such a description is derived, circulated, understood, and accepted by the client constituency, the instructional supervisor must carry out the outlined tasks and accept accountability for their effectiveness.

The supervisor's role encompasses three basic leadership components: administrative, curricular, and instructional. It is difficult if not impossible to view these as mutually exclusive functions of the supervisor's or instructional supervisor's role. In fact, it may not be desirable to completely separate them.

As administrator, the supervisor arranges schedules, as well as plans, implements, and keeps records necessary for effective operation. The supervisor must have a curriculum knowledge base, whether subject-specific (at a specific level or all-level) or subject-comprehensive (again, at a specific level or all-level). The supervisor must also have a firm foundation in instruction and in analysis of instruction. While realizing that general supervisors may not have the degree of skills necessary to be instructional leaders, we prefer that all supervisors be, some to a larger degree than others, instructional leaders.

Let us for the moment accept that supervision includes all those ingredients mentioned, and represent them in a Venn diagram by the universal set U. All activities not curricular or administrative, but instead related to instructional supervision, will be represented by subset A of the universal set U. We can further subdivide the space represented in subset A by referring to all of the activities of clinical supervision in the subset B. Figure 1 thus helps us to see that of all things a supervisor does, only those in space B involve direct, in-class, and/or face-to-face instruction-related contacts.

FIGURE 1

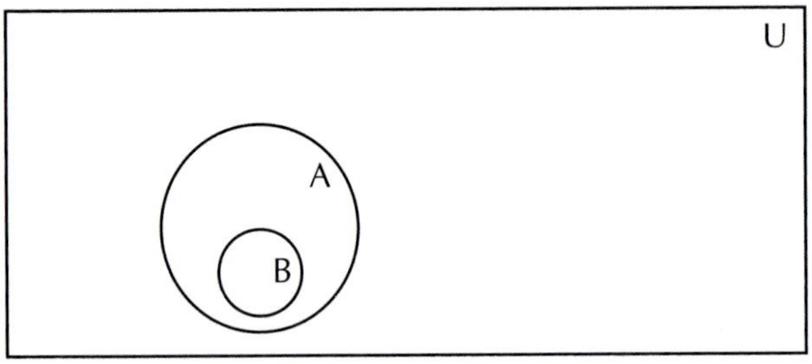

U = All types of supervision
A = Instructional supervision
B = Clinical supervision

The proportions shown may or may not be realistic or typical, and we hope that many readers will protest that, in their own experience, A and B are larger parts of U than the figure suggests. That is well and good. We would like to suggest that Figure 2 comes closer to an ideal at which American education ought to aim:

FIGURE 2

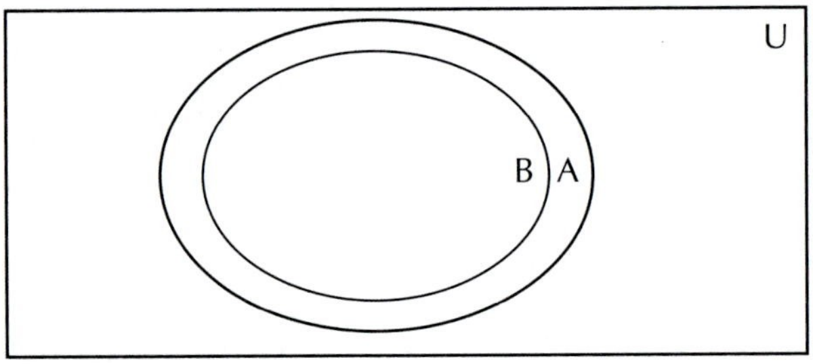

U = All types of supervision
A = Instructional supervision
B = Clinical supervision

Figure 1 suggests that, first of all, instructional supervision probably does not comprise even a third of all supervision; rather, its total is relegated to a smaller amount or proportion of the whole. As previously noted, instructional supervision's role is still ambiguous, and often persons who serve in that role are not free to actuate the kinds of activities they feel necessary to fulfill it. We also opine that with better preparation programs for supervisors, and more emphasis on instructional improvement procedures within these programs, instructional supervision will assume a greater role within supervision. Should this happen (and much indicates that it will and is beginning to do so), clinical supervision's role in the school will be closer to the ideal shown in Figure 2.

In the grandest of all ideals, A (instructional supervision) equals B (clinical supervision), which would be characterized as an elliptical subset tangential to each side of the rectangle U. If A = B = tangential to U, then CS maximizes its benefit for improving instruction.

SUMMARY

■ Supervision is an integral dimension of leadership. Throughout education endeavor for the past two decades, the focus on supervising has shifted from its use as *a monitoring activity* to its value in *human resource development.* The popular theme is to make it possible for people to develop and use their talents. CS, which has been moving steadily in that direction from its inception, is an especially valuable approach to helping individuals and their organizations to thrive. As people talk about management, they talk about empowerment. CS is letting people use the power they have.

CS has its roots in leadership. The qualities for successful leadership in fields such as business and medicine, described in this chapter, are similar to the qualities needed by supervisors. Perhaps the medical clinic best described what Robert Goldhammer thought of as he pictured his ideal school setting—in which "staff" and "residents" work side by side, learning from one another as they provide the best possible learning situation for each student.

REFERENCES

[1] "The Fourth Yearbook of the Department of Supervisors and Directors of Instruction of the National Education Association," *Evaluation of Supervision*, Teachers College Press, New York, 1931, p. 3.

[2] Robert H. Anderson, "Presumption of Competence," *National Forum of Educational Administration and Supervision Journal 7*, 1990–91, pp. 101–110.

[3] Ibid.

[4] William H. Lucio and John D. McNeil, *Supervision in Thought and Action*, 3rd ed., McGraw-Hill, New York, 1979, p.3.

[5] Daniel L. Duke, *School Leadership and Instructional Improvement*, Random House, New York, 1987.

[6] Carter V. Good, *Dictionary of Education*, 3rd ed., McGraw-Hill, New York, 1973, p. 574.

[7] John T. Lovell and Kimball Wiles, *Supervision for Better Schools*, 5th ed., Prentice-Hall, Englewood Cliffs, N.J., 1983, p. 4.

[8] Laurel J. Tanner, "Eighty-Seventh Yearbook of the National Society for the Study of Curriculum, Part 1," *Critical Issues in Curriculum*, University of Chicago Press, Chicago, 1988.

[9] R.L. Andrews and R. Soder, *Educational Leadership*, 1987, 44:9–11.

ADDITIONAL REFERENCES

A Nation at Risk: The Imperative for Educational Reform, U.S. Government Printing Office, Washington, D.C., 1983.

National Commission on Excellence in Education, *A Nation at Risk: The Full Account*, ed. by USA Research Staff, U.S.A. Research, Inc., Portland, Oregon, 1984.

CHAPTER

3

A Model Of Clinical Supervision

In This Chapter

- A Framework of Values
- The Model
- Teaming: A Vital Ingredient
- A Conceptual Background
- Summary

We believe that the concept of clinical supervision has enriched and expanded the overall field of supervision and helped to expose the naivete and the general inadequacy of prior definitions and role recommendations. We think that supervisors have too long been misled into believing that they could keep profitably busy without spending much time in classrooms. If this seems a harsh criticism, let the reader consult the usual textbook to see how many pages deal with direct classroom-based involvement. Our role in this volume is to tilt the supervisor's interests in the direction of such involvement, and to redefine the role of the supervisor accordingly.

Thus this chapter begins with a framework of values and aims for supervision, followed by derivation and explanation of the Goldhammer five-stage clinical supervision operational model. Teaming, an integral component of the original clinical supervision work at Harvard, and a practice which seems to be gathering momentum via the school restructuring movement, is also presented. The conceptual background of clinical supervision, which describes the "whys" of the clinical supervision idea and model, is then discussed. The summary is an overview outline of the CS model, with purposes for each of the five stages.

A FRAMEWORK OF VALUES

■ Our ideas and practice of CS arise from a framework of values in connection to which the discipline acquires its purposes and its rationales. We value certain educational priorities that are reflected in most of the literature of innovative practice since the mid-1950s. We are driven by images of teaching that enhance the learners' self-sufficiency, and of supervision that facilitates such teaching and aims for a parallel condition in the teacher's own existence.

We value learning that focuses upon its own processes and structures. We value inquiry, analysis, examination, and evaluation, especially when such activities of the mind are self-initiated and self-regulated. We believe that supervision facilitating such outcomes must be inherently humane, conceptually tough, grounded in intellectual humility, and based upon a determination to discover more about reality.

The supervision we envisage is intended to increase teachers' incentives and skills for self-supervision and for supervising their professional colleagues. It is additionally intended to become progressively more useful as teachers become increasingly capable of employing it creatively. We imagine, in other words, a supervision that becomes more and more productive as the teacher achieves higher and higher levels of technical and professional sophistication, most notably the ability to reach out for the special provisions that CS incorporates potentially. Our minds struggle for images of a supervision whose principal effect is to expand the sense of gratification experienced by students, teachers, and supervisors, gratification in being and gratification in the work they do.

The aims of clinical supervision will be realized when, largely by virtue of its own existence, everyone inside the school will know better why he or she is there, will want to be there, will be concerned with important curriculum questions, and will feel a strong and beautiful awareness of his or her own individual identity, and a spirit of community and enterprise with colleagues. These are the values that motivate our work and give rise to our ambitions. Although we cannot, obviously, make promises that are as large as our dreams, we can proclaim those dreams and let ourselves be guided by them.

In its present stage of development, the clinical supervision that our minds can formulate and that we seek to practice does not completely fulfill the ideal that occupies our imaginations. Day by day we know better what it is, in life and in professional life, that we are after. And, by small increments, we are getting to know better how to get what we are after. The following model of clinical supervision and the writing that surrounds it are mainly an expression of our trials.

THE MODEL

■ As we turn to discussion of our basic five-stage model, it may be helpful to acknowledge that ours is only one of several models designed to accomplish essentially the same purposes. As participants in, or at least as intrigued observers of, the early stages of model development at Harvard University, Anderson and Goldhammer engaged in events that at first involved working with graduate students preparing for teaching careers and soon involved working with experienced teachers, principals, and others being trained to work in teaching-team projects. Known as the Harvard-Lexington Summer Program (HLSP), the ultimate setting within which the five-stage "cycle of supervision," or "ob cycle," evolved in their experience was one over which Anderson had a major directing responsibility and in which Goldhammer served as a junior faculty member. In those days Cogan's ideas provided the basic foundations, and in fact Cogan was a part of HLSP (which was operated in the summers of 1961, 1962, 1963, 1964, and in Boston in 1965) in the first year or two. Goldhammer, on whose doctoral committee Anderson served and who later worked with Cogan at the University of Pittsburgh, did his dissertation on the topic of clinical supervision; and the appearance of his 1969 volume (of which this book is the third edition) represented a major event in the literature.

In HLSP, teams of trainees spent alternate weeks under faculty supervision in team curriculum planning, in team teaching (carrying out the plan), and in team observations of the teaching being done by fellow trainees. The observation activities, as it turned out, were remarkably more exciting, more dramatic, and more educative for the trainees than were the other two phases of the training cycle; and, in fact, some of the offshoot training programs (for example, IGE [Individually Guided Education] clinical workshops) have telescoped the planning and teaching phases so that more trainee energy can go into the ob cycle.

The 1969 Goldhammer description of the ob cycle followed the eventual HLSP pattern, which embraced five stages. In his 1973 text Cogan[1] presented the cycle in eight phases, the first three of which (establishing the teacher-supervisor relationship, and planning with the teacher) correspond with Goldhammer's Stage 1, and two others of which (analyzing the teaching-learning process, and planning the strategy of the conference) correspond with Goldhammer's Stage 3. Cogan's final phase (Number 8, renewed planning) treats the post-observation activity in a way somewhat different from Goldhammer's, but it seems reasonable to claim that there are no major differences in the structure of the cycle of supervision as described by the two authors. This is not to deny that the two authors make unique and somewhat different contributions, however.

In the subsequent editions of Goldhammer's work, we keep the five-stage description largely to update and reinforce, rather than drastically alter, Goldhammer's views. Because of our admiration for Cogan's treatment of the topic, however, we suggest that many readers will want to consult his presentation as well as our own.

The basic CS model consists of five stages:

1. Pre-observation conference,
2. Observation,
3. Analysis and strategy,
4. Supervision conference, and
5. Post-conference analysis.

Stage 1: The Pre-Observation Conference

This stage is mainly intended to provide a mental and procedural framework for the remainder of the cycle. Although its functions can be viewed somewhat differently by the teacher and the supervisor, in general, in our practice, it has served the following purposes:

Confirming and Nurturing the Teacher-Supervisor Relationship Both supervisor and teacher, through the trust already earned and the history already recorded, will begin to feel comfortable with each other to form the basis for productive supervision.

Fluency Both the teacher and the supervisor require a fluent identification of the teacher's concerns about instruction and a translation of those concerns into procedures for improving the teacher's instruction. The better the teacher knows his or her self-improvement goals, the better they can be implemented. The principal means, in this stage, for enhancing both members' fluency, is for the teacher to present his or her most polished and updated version of plans for the observed lesson. That presentation serves dual purposes: the supervisor learns just what the teacher has in mind, and the teacher is able to test and increase self-fluency by verbalizing ideas to the supervisor.

Rehearsal The simple enunciation of plans provides the teacher with at least a conceptual rehearsal or role-play of possible problem areas of the lesson, such as the teacher's key questions or unanticipated student responses. Such problems for rehearsal may arise from either the teacher's or the supervisor's concerns and may be initiated by either member in the pre-observation conference.

Revisions Complementing rehearsal is the opportunity for last-minute revisions in the lesson plan.

Agreement The pre-observation conference is a time for the teacher and the supervisor to agree about reasons for supervision to occur in the immediate situation and about how supervision should operate. When certain rules have been decided upon—"This is what you will do, this is what I will do, and here's why"—generally they should not be changed in the middle of the game except by mutual consent and understanding.

Stage 2: Observation

The supervisor observes the lesson so that he or she may analyze it with the teacher afterward. Toward this end, data are recorded in appropriate ways. Whether analysis will be centered on problems identified beforehand (in Stage 1) or will emerge freshly from the new data, it is crucially important that the data constitute as true, as accurate, and as complete a representation of what took place as possible to provide a sound basis for planning future teaching.

Today's data are employed as a source of tomorrow's agenda for supervision. One reason for the supervisor to observe is that the teacher, being engaged in the business of teaching, cannot usually see the same things happening that a disengaged observer can. By adding eyes, technology, and objective analysis instruments, the data are increased. Another reason is to demonstrate commitment to the teacher, a serious enough commitment to justify paying such close attention to his or her behavior as the observer must.

Another rationale for Stage 2 is that by being in close proximity to teacher and pupils at the very moments when salient problems of professional practice are being enacted, the supervisor occupies a position from which to render real assistance to the teacher, in the teacher's terms, and according to specific observational foci and instrumentation agreed upon in Stage 1.

In a general sense, observation should create opportunities for supervisors to help teachers test reality, the reality of their own perceptions and judgments about their teaching. We argue that supervision should result in heightened autonomy for the teacher and, particularly, in strengthened capacities for independent, objective self-analysis: given the supervisor's own perceptions of what has taken place, the teacher can test "reality" by ascertaining whether the supervisor's observations tend to confirm or to oppose his or her own.

Stage 3: Analysis and Strategy

Stage 3 has two general purposes: first, in analysis, to make observational data intelligible and manageable; and second, in strategy, to plan the management of the supervision conference to follow—that is, to determine what issues to treat, which data to cite, what goals to aim for, how to begin, where to end, and who should do what.

If, as we have suggested, observation is a fundamental element in clinical supervision, then analysis is its heart. In a very real sense, it is also its brain: of all the activities within the cycle, thinking analytically about what was observed and coming to an understanding of the issues, questions, and principles that are involved, is an exceedingly demanding intellectual task. Rationales for analysis can be formulated either historically or methodologically. Historically, supervision has been deeply entrenched in evaluation (rating) and at times without much objective evidence. A rationale for extensive analysis of empirical data in supervision is that teachers' anxieties and mistrust of supervision can be alleviated only if teachers learn that supervision is (or can be) an essentially rational practice, that its methods are those of logical reasoning and forthright analysis.

The analytical component of clinical supervision is intended to make it safer—less opinion-driven, less arbitrary, less superficial—than supervision of the past. And particularly when the teacher is trained to participate in the teaching analysis, based on true comprehensive representations of that teaching, his or her chances of benefitting from the enterprise are most favorable. We argue that for most teachers, analysis of their teaching should be the most useful thing that anyone else can do in relation to it.

Methodologically, analysis exists for the sake of understanding today's teaching in order to modify tomorrow's teaching. Analysis provides possibilities for the teacher to be vigorously engaged in self-examination of teaching and be more independent in framing decisions that affect the teaching.

The supervisor's next step, after having performed an analysis of the observational data, is to make decisions about how the supervision conference should be conducted. The principal rationale for strategy, like that for instructional planning, is that a planned approach toward specified goals by deliberate processes is more likely to work out than a random one. If supervision is intended to result in process outcomes as well as in purely technical ones, that is, if it is intended to affect patterns of behavior and underlying psychological predispositions as well as simply to transmit substantive information, then it is more difficult to prepare for supervision than it would be otherwise. Both technical and process outcomes depend very much upon one another. We must prepare in several integrated dimensions; and strategy is the time for doing so, if we conceptualize supervision in these terms.

Stage 4: The Supervision Conference

All roads lead to the conference. Whereas it is sometimes appropriate to omit earlier stages of the clinical cycle for special reasons, and whereas even on certain occasions shortages of time may preclude any supervisory contact except a conference, once a sequence has been begun it is almost never acceptable to abandon it before the conference. Some kind of conference is almost always preferable to no conference at all. In our work with supervision students in professional practicums, Rule Number 1 is, generally, "Stay out of the classroom unless you are committed to a full sequence of supervision. Your participation in a conference is what earns you your right to observe." The supervision conference is additionally intended to:

1. Indicate to the teacher that the supervisor has a genuine and enduring interest in what goes on in the classroom, thereby providing incentive for teacher improvement.

2. Provide a time to redefine the supervisory agreement in order to decide what directions supervision should take and by what methods it should operate.

3. Provide a time to plan future teaching in collaboration with another professional educator.

4. Define treatable issues in the teaching and authenticate the existence of issues that have been sensed intuitively.

5. Offer didactic assistance to the teacher, either directly or by referral, in relation to information or theory that the teacher requires and of which the supervisor may have relatively advanced knowledge.

6. Train the teacher in techniques for self-supervision and develop incentives for professional self-analysis.

Stage 5: The Post-Conference Analysis

The conference analysis arises from pragmatic, methodological, and historical considerations. First, it is a basis for assessing whether supervision is working productively, for ascertaining its strengths and weaknesses, and for modifying supervisory practices accordingly. Second, the supervisor can demonstrate skills of self-analysis by familiarizing the teacher with the work to be done in the post-conference analysis, perhaps by videotaping it for analysis by the teacher afterward. Third, the teacher's awareness of the supervisor's post-conference analysis should help to offset misgivings that may exist concerning the supervisor's commitment and the historical disparity between his or her professional vulnerability and the teacher's.

In essence, the conference analysis serves as clinical supervision's superego—its conscience. It is the time when the supervisor's practice is examined with all of the rigor and for basically the same purposes that the teacher's was—that is, for improvement of supervision, and ultimately instruction. According to this view, decisions affecting the conduct of our future behavior must arise, in large part, from objective analysis of our past behavior and from as fine an understanding as we can develop of what consequences it has had.

For a summary outline of the CS cycle, see the appendix on pages 175–176, "The Clinical Supervision Cycle: An Overview."

TEAMING: A VITAL INGREDIENT

■ One of the most important concepts related to the successful implementation of CS is that there should be at least a sense of partnership, and at best a true working relationship, between the parties involved. In most of the discussion of CS in this volume, the implication is that the supervisor occupies a superordinate (or equivalent leadership) position which includes the official responsibility for working with, and helping, teachers in the classroom. We are eager, however, to alert the reader early on to our enthusiasm for arrangements which enable classroom teachers, as peers, to "supervise" each other in a collegial setting. Of these, the most elaborate and also the most powerful are those described by the term "team teaching."

If we had the power and authority to do so, we would eliminate the literal self-contained classroom as a feature of the American school scene, and develop in its place many varieties of team teaching. From our viewpoint, teachers whose everyday working situation calls for direct collaboration and attendant interchanges have a tremendous professional advantage over teachers who work in isolation. For example, we believe that teachers in teams, especially when they experience the conditions described below, have the great privilege of reacting to, and learning from, each other in ways that self-contained teachers simply cannot duplicate. We believe that the best way to insure a collegial atmosphere in schools, of the sort that is now so widely advocated in the literature, is to move into a team structure. We believe that CS, as a mechanism for helping teachers to thrive professionally, can reach its highest potential within such a structure.

It therefore seems appropriate at this point to discuss the history, features, and promise of team teaching. Our hope is that reader awareness of this information will lead to a better understanding of the role that CS could play in their professional lives.

First, a little history. Although John Dewey's disciples took virtually no subsequent notice of the fact, the Dewey Laboratory School at the University of Chicago around the turn of the century embraced the concept under the label of "cooperative social organization."[2]

It was not, however, until the late 1950s that the idea of team teaching was developed and tested. During the 1960s and early 1970s there emerged many (perhaps hundreds of) team teaching models, a number of which remain more or less in place today. Generally regarded as one of the most powerful and promising of the so-called innovations in those turbulent decades, teaming was also one of the most controversial. The chief reason for the lively, sometimes furious debates about teaming was that there was very strong, albeit unfounded, faith in the self-contained classroom as a presumably ideal environment for young children. It took more than a decade of research and experience to counteract such faith and to develop theoretical and conceptual support for the teaming alternative.

Gradually the debate subsided, and at present it can be sagely claimed that there is no body of research, or even of well-informed opinion, in support of the self-contained classroom as a preferred arrangement. To the contrary, all the evidence known to us confirms that both teachers and children are much better served within a team framework. Yet in the 1990s by far the most prevalent organizational structure in American schools remains the self-contained classroom. How could this be?

One of your authors (see Anderson, 1988) has attempted to explain why acceptance and development of team teaching has been so slow.[3] We can list a dozen reasons:

1. In the early years, the idea became a bandwagon much too fast, and too many claims and promises were made that were slow to be fulfilled.
2. Advocates underestimated the difficulty and cost, especially in human effort, of making such a dramatic change in the lives of people whose past loyalties to self-containment often ran very deep.
3. Opponents characterized teaming as a serious professional heresy, strongly at variance with established beliefs, habits, and customs associated with self-containment.
4. Prominent professors of education and others active in professional publications and organizations reacted in a hostile manner, emphasizing that teaming was a probable threat to the well-being of young children.
5. Nearly 100% of existing school buildings utilized the familiar "egg-crate" design with rows of equal-sized insulated classrooms, and these did not provide a flexible setting within which team teaching could be easily attempted.
6. Typical preparation programs for teachers, supervisors, and administrators paid almost no attention to equipping adults to work together in groups, set common goals, solve group problems, or deal with organizational dynamics. Furthermore, the available and relevant knowledge base on these topics, while not exactly primitive, was not usually included in teacher-education courses.
7. Team teaching has a somewhat glamorous and venturesome flavor that attracted foundation money and also attracted the interest of venturesome superintendents, some of whom unfortunately launched team-teaching projects by edict or without sufficient thought about the complexities involved.
8. Very few of the teachers and principals who were involved in launching a team-teaching project were given a sufficient amount, if any, of prior training to assure a successful launch.
9. Similarly, few projects were provided with sufficient resources (flexible space, consultant assistance, released time, aides, and so forth) to insure success and continuation.
10. Inordinate time and energy went into defending the pilot projects, persuading parents and community leaders to accept and support them, and tending to problems caused by mistakes and misunderstandings in a trial-and-error atmosphere.

11. Principals, teachers and team leaders in visible and successful projects were recruited aggressively by other school districts, and these "experts" soon became upwardly mobile. This caused a brain-and-talent drain that destroyed staff stability and continuity at the leadership level in many projects.
12. In addition, the heavy staff turnover characteristic of most American schools took its usual toll, and replacement personnel generally brought with them an orientation to the traditional self-contained classroom.

A very favorable atmosphere now appears to exist for renewed efforts to embrace and utilize teaming arrangements. Since the mid-1980s, the term *restructuring* has been widely used as a label for the changes that must be made if American schools are to fulfill their societal role. Almost without exception, discussions of restructuring either imply or indicate straight-out that teachers must work more closely together. Terms such as site-based management, bottom-up decision making, work-culture building, differentiated staffing, instructional support teams, interdisciplinary instruction, flexible scheduling, collegial interaction, and collaboration are abundant in the literature and in public discussions of needed reforms.

Murphy provided a very helpful review of the movement to restructure schools and of the skills and understandings that teachers and school leaders will need in order to succeed within the new arrangements.[4]

Noting the many changes that are likely to happen in the process of teaching within restructured schools, Murphy observes that there will be greater reliance on interactive and cooperative instructional strategies, more emphasis on depth in the curriculum and less reliance on traditional organizational arrangements. He states that teachers "need to develop skills that enable them to be productive members of organizational teams," and that restructured schools will provide teachers with expanded and more challenging opportunities to interact with their colleagues, and to develop understanding and skill in collegial decision making. Collegial interaction and collaboration, he observes, will become the norm rather than anomalies in restructured schools.

Murphy indicates further that in the light of increased adult interactions, teachers will need to develop a rich understanding of theories, conceptual frameworks and models of conflict resolution, leadership, communication, and decision making. They will have to learn how to overcome the constraints imposed by such common organizational arrangements as the self-contained classroom, the 50-minute period, and the standard curriculum. His concluding sentence notes that if teaching and learning are to be improved, prospective teachers must have the knowledge and skills to work more effectively with their peers and students.

We agree with this analysis, and we perceive that whatever gains are made in preparing teachers to work together will also lead to immediate gains in the amount as well as the quality of professional conversation that we would associate with CS.

Teaming: One Definition

Any arrangement that calls for significant, continuous professional collaboration might legitimately be called team teaching. However, we think that the best way to enjoy the full advantages of teaming would be to adopt a pattern within which these six features are prominent:

1. Long-range as well as short-range curriculum planning, including occasional group review of each teacher's specific lesson plans, is a total group responsibility.
2. The team members, although much of their teaching is done within a "solo" or private context, regularly work together (co-teach).
3. The pupils, although connected for advisory and other purposes to one or another of the teachers, belong to and are regularly connected with all of the teaching team members.
4. Assessment of each child's progress and needs is an activity in which all team members participate in some systematic manner.
5. Assessment of the instructional program, overall as well as components with which individual teachers are concerned, is a teamwide responsibility.
6. Resources of all kinds (space, equipment, materials, books, and other paraphernalia) are shared (co-owned) for the benefit of all.

We believe that when all six of these features are in place, teachers are in an especially favorable position to not only deal with the full range of instructional problems but also to expand and enrich their professional knowledge and skill base. In the best sense, teachers in such a setting have the privilege of participation in what amounts to a non-stop graduate-level seminar, 180 or so days a year. No doubt such persons will also find that their lives and their calendars are very full, with considerable frustration about the speed with which the clock moves each day; but most will conclude that there is a good trade-off in the excitement and stimulation that teaming generates.

The CS model, having great adaptability potential, can be used in a variety of ways to improve instruction, particularly in the team-teaching classroom. Observation cycles, sometimes full-fledged and sometimes in abbreviated form, can be built into a team's daily and weekly schedules. Being so intimately connected with each other, team teachers rapidly lose the self-consciousness and anxiety that often afflict self-contained teachers when a CS cycle is imminent. The more open, collaborative, non-defensive CS approach leads to an increased sense of productivity and satisfaction by the teacher. The offering of constructive criticism becomes a welcome message from a colleague, and the levels of professional conversation in the team context can become very high. Experience and research strongly suggest, however, that for such sharing practices to emerge, the building principal and others in supervisory or administrative roles must:

1. Have great understanding not only of team teaching but of the CS observation cycle.
2. Possess and manifest a strong personal commitment to the improvement of teaching and to the use of CS as a professional tool.
3. Provide resources and time, and actually work CS into the busy schedule of the school.

Such understandings and commitments are likelier to exist if the supervisors have a strong conceptual grasp of CS and its elements.

A CONCEPTUAL BACKGROUND

■ Before going further, it may be helpful to examine some of the concepts associated with the term *clinical supervision.* Already evident is that clinical supervision is a subcategory of the general term *supervision* as it is commonly used in education to indicate all of the activities, functions, maneuvers, and nurturing conditions that are intended to help teachers (and various other educational workers) to upgrade their performance. The adjective *clinical,* which was appropriated from other sciences for education in about 1958 by Morris Cogan,[5] conveys the idea that such efforts are based upon data collected in actual classroom (or other instructional) situations where the teacher is working directly with the learners and the supervisor is present. In the "clinic" of the classroom, the supervisor obtains a more accurate and complete understanding of what actually occurs. In the succeeding events, to pursue the clinical analogy, the supervisor and teacher meet face-to-face to review those occurrences and their import.

We associate at least nine characteristics or notions with the practice of clinical supervision:

1. It is a technology for improving instruction.
2. It is a deliberate intervention into the instructional process.
3. It is goal-oriented combining the school needs with the personal growth needs of those who work within the school.
4. It assumes a professional working relationship between teacher(s) and supervisor(s).

5. It requires a high degree of mutual trust, as reflected in understanding, support, and commitment for growth.

6. It is systematic, although it requires a flexible and continuously changing methodology.

7. It creates productive (i.e., healthy) tension for bridging the gap between the real and the ideal.

8. It assumes that the supervisor knows a great deal about the analysis of instruction and learning and also about productive human interaction.

9. It requires both pre-service training, especially in observation techniques, and continuous in-service reflection on effective approaches.

It has already been noted that CS can and should happen, frequently, within a peer context. We think, however, that it remains appropriate to discuss CS within the more familiar framework of role-related supervision in which a person with appropriate skills and background seeks to help classroom teachers from the viewpoint of a "teacher of teachers."

Briefly stated, teaching calls for expertise with respect to at least three skill categories:

1. Command of and commitment to the content of the school curriculum,

2. Understanding of the relationships that can and should exist between teachers and their students, and

3. Understanding of the many dimensions of teaching and learning.

Stated another way, the teacher has to have a good feel for working with kids, a strong repertoire of instructional skills, and a strong knowledge base in what (for lack of a better term) is usually called the "content."

While this may not be an adequate definition of what teachers need to know and do, let us go on to say that the supervisor, in order to be effective and authentic, ought in every case to be an exemplar. Anyone who does not know how to relate to kids, who has not been a successful manager of the teaching-learning enterprise, and who is not obviously in good command of (one or more) content areas will not be easily accepted as qualified to offer advice and counsel. Equally important is that a deficiency in any of those skill areas would render the supervisor much less capable of recognizing and dealing intellectually with deficiencies on the part of persons being observed.

Beyond being an exemplar, however, are the skills a supervisor needs as a teacher of teachers. A thorough understanding of teaching is a good foundation; necessary, too, is the ability to work with adults whose task role is teaching and whose goal is to grow toward greater proficiency in that role. In much the same way that teachers are obliged to diagnose and relate to their pupils, the supervisor must be able to diagnose and relate to teachers. In much the same way that teachers must develop a repertoire of instructional skills for use with their pupils, the supervisor must develop a repertoire of skills for use with teachers. And, in much the same way that teachers must have great command of the curriculum and its elements, the supervisor must have great command of the teacher's professional curriculum, namely how to carry out the role of a teacher with skill and distinction.

Are we saying that the supervisor must actually be a "more perfect" teacher than the people with whom he or she works? No, that would not be realistic—nor is it in fact essential. It is conceivable that many teachers will be more "perfect" than their supervisor with respect to overall classroom performance. What matters is that the supervisor would be sufficiently skilled so that the teachers' skill level can be recognized and appreciated, and also so that intelligent questions and suggestions can be raised.

Are we saying that the supervisor must always be a master of the subject matter or content being examined? Here our answer has two aspects. First of all, we believe that there are innumerable generic dimensions of teaching about which there can always be profitable discussion. In more familiar terms, we have no doubt that a supervisor in a secondary school can be a useful observer/supervisor for every teacher in the school regardless of that teacher's specialty. Secondly, however, we acknowledge that good supervision must go beyond the generic and be concerned with the content. Being unfamiliar with the content need not interfere with the asking of helpful questions about that content, but there are times when content-specific questions and problems arise and the supervisory function must involve someone with content expertise. At these times, either the supervisory task should be turned over to such an expert, or (preferably, in our view) an expert should be invited to participate alongside the generalist supervisor, in one or more cycles as appropriate.

SUMMARY

Overview Outline: Clinical Supervision Model

Stage I: Pre-Observation Conference

- Confirm and nurture the teacher-supervisor relationship.
- Identify teacher's needs and concerns, and develop means to address them.

- Provide a conceptual rehearsal for lesson problem areas.
- Ensure an agreement for rationale and method of observation.

Stage II: Observation

- Observe the lesson and obtain objective data on determined foci.

Stage III: Analysis and Strategy

- Reconstruct observed events as objectively as possible.
- Sort and relate these events to the determined foci.
- Review data thoroughly, analyze noteworthy patterns of the teacher's behavior, and consider supervisory implications.
- Plan a strategy for the conference.
- Look ahead to future teacher growth and development.

Stage IV: Supervisory Conference

- Define and confirm teaching issues through lesson feedback.
- Provide didactic help for improving future teaching.
- Provide training in techniques of teacher self-improvement.

Stage V: Post-Conference Analysis

- Reconstruct, as appropriate, the events of the conference.
- Assess the conference in terms of:

  —teacher's criteria, as determined in the pre-observation conference;

  —supervisory criteria;

  —apparent value of the conference to the teacher.
- Evaluate the supervisor's skill in handling the several stages of the cycle.

REFERENCES

[1] Morris Cogan, *Clinical Supervision*, Houghton Mifflin, Boston, 1973.

[2] Robert H. Anderson, "John Dewey on Supervision (and Related Matters)" *Florida ASCD Journal 5*, Spring 1989, pp. 13–17.

[3] Robert H. Anderson, "Team Teaching: Quo Vadis?," *Florida ASCD Journal 5*, Fall 1988, pp. 17–22.

[4] Joseph Murphy, "Helping Teachers Prepare to Work In Restructured Schools," *Journal of Teacher Education 41*, September–October 1990, pp. 50–56.

[5] Morris Cogan, *Clinical Supervision*, Houghton Mifflin, Boston, 1973.

CHAPTER

4

Setting The Stage For Clinical Supervision

In This Chapter

- Facilitating Success
- Collaboration
- Peer Supervision
- Morale
- Rapport
- Self-Acceptance
- Rapport Nurturance
- Summary

This chapter presents rationale and prerequisites for clinical supervision success. Eleven CS facilitating conditions are listed; Conditions 1 through 5 are explored in this chapter, and the remaining six in forthcoming chapters as appropriate. Next, traditional and collaborative supervisory styles are compared. Then peer supervision, a natural concomitant of teaching, is explained. The importance of the supervisor's role in teacher morale, supervisor-teacher rapport, and supervisor-teacher self-acceptance follows. Lastly, practical rapport nurturance techniques are offered.

FACILITATING SUCCESS

■ Setting the stage for clinical supervision is crucial for success. It is necessary to get off to a good start by ensuring that a positive, caring, and mutually comfortable relationship exists between the supervisor/coach and the teacher. But good feelings and comfortable relationships do not always develop swiftly or automatically, and sometimes it takes a while before the teacher feels secure enough to engage in a CS relationship. We feel CS has eleven facilitating conditions, the first five of which are essential to setting the stage, and the remaining six are integral to specific stages of the observation cycle. They are:

1. Specific, achievement-oriented, school-wide improvement goals are in place.
2. Teacher has immediate as well as long-range objectives for strengthening own classroom performance.
3. A growth plan (with target objective, a timeline, and progress checks) has been established.
4. Supervisor/coach and teacher understand each other and the work context; interpersonal decoding is not necessary.
5. "The past is prologue"; previous episodes provide background.
6. Pre-observation agreement is respected as a contract.

7. Observer's presence is minimally distracting to students.

8. Observer's apperceptive skills and data-gathering tools are employed at full speed.

9. Observer postpones judgments or conclusions until an objective basis is established.

10. Post-observation conference is a professional conversation, a privileged moment to stretch for deeper understandings.

11. Post-conference analysis is a new and different event.

Facilitating Condition 1

Specific, achievement-oriented, school-wide improvement goals should be in place. Having helped define the goals, and presumably possessing some enthusiasm for them, each teacher then has a kind of "curriculum compass" serving as a guide to select personal goal tasks.

Facilitating Condition 2

Within the school goals, *teachers must have defined immediate and long-range objectives for strengthening their own classroom performance, within the school goals.* Clinical supervision should not be an overwhelming experience. While teacher growth needs may vary, it is helpful to concentrate on but a few professional improvement goals in which coaching/supervision focuses with in-depth attention over a period of months if not the entire year.

Facilitating Condition 3

The teacher must establish, with the supervisor, a growth plan for the year, with target objective(s), a timeline, and progress checks. Thinking through the tasks and breaking them into manageable segments helps both the teacher and supervisor gain a better understanding of goals and processes in question.

> [T]he supervisory program is the nervous system of the school. It is, above all else, the mechanism for adaptation; it represents that ability to adapt to new conditions which an organism—or school—must have or die.[1]

The supervisory aspect of any school system is vital to the success that system has in producing a top-quality educational network in which teachers and students interact and grow. One may liken curriculum to a sport, and the skill and technique used in that sport to instructional effectiveness. Within any sport, the proper equipment occupies an important role; yet we know that equipment alone is hardly sufficient for success. A knowledge base of the sport and its rules is necessary, as well as skill in application of that knowledge base.

Consider the sport of golf. Owning an excellent set of clubs, using the finest golf balls, and wearing a top-notch pair of golf shoes cannot guarantee one a quality golf game. Acquisition and maintenance of skills is necessary. Even the best professional tour golfers must, from time to time (and some on a regular basis) seek the help of a master analyst/teacher/coach to work out their swing problems, sharpen their game, and regain self-confidence, thus allowing them to maintain skills necessary to retain their status on the tour.

Now consider a school. It may be housed in a well-designed building, contain the latest equipment in its classrooms and labs, and possess an excellent curriculum. However, without teachers who seek continual professional growth to improve their teaching techniques and skills in working with students, the school may not excel, in either achievement of pupils or reputation for professionalism.

Like the professional golfer, the teacher must have a knowledge base and the skills necessary to implement that knowledge successfully. Just as professional golfers must periodically seek help to sharpen their skills, so must teachers. Golfers turn to an advisor they trust; likewise, teachers turn to a supervisor they trust.

Analogies between other professionals and teachers reveal that the *most* skillful persons, in fact, may well be the ones most eager for further improvement and therefore for further counsel. We are reminded of the legendary Ted Williams, of the Boston Red Sox, who never ceased to be an ardent student of batsmanship and who, even at the peak of his career, constantly discussed the science of hitting with top players, coaches, and retired baseball stars.

So it should be with teachers. There is probably no more desirable attribute in professional teachers than an eagerness to improve their teaching methods, approaches, and content for the students. Clinical supervision makes this possible because, in it, instructional improvement is an ongoing procedure. Morris Cogan succeeds in capturing the nature of clinical supervision when he says, "Clinical supervision does not mean that the teacher is in training. It means that he is continually engaged in improving his practice, as is required of all professionals."[2]

To the teacher who is motivated, clinical supervision makes available the teaching professional who can be of direct assistance and who draws upon a fund of knowledge about the best way to "hit the ball." The advisors/coaches, furthermore, base their responses and suggestions upon data gathered directly from the classroom, and they use techniques to analyze data and provide feedback that will contribute not only to methodological/instructional improvements but also to the teacher's well-being.

The well-qualified and well-motivated clinical supervisor uses techniques that have nearly universal applicability. Yet no supervisor can have a strong background in all curriculum subjects, nor is it likely that most will have extensive training and experience at all levels of schooling (pre-school, elementary, middle school, secondary, and post-secondary). This means that certain kinds of questions may be more challenging to some supervisors than others. We recognize that. However, we believe that most clinical supervision techniques are relevant to the whole gamut of educational situations, and that a skillful supervisor can work successfully with any teacher of any subject at any level. One need not be a master of physics to help transform a mediocre physics teacher into a good one through an analysis of classroom dynamics. Similarly, a former physics teacher, childless and largely ignorant about five-year-olds, may prove enormously helpful to a kindergarten teacher in such domains as interaction, curriculum content, communications, and lesson pacing.

We hope this argument will reduce the resistance that teachers, perhaps especially at the secondary level, sometimes offer when they perceive that the supervisor comes from a background different from their own. Secondary teachers tend, more than elementary teachers, to be heavily committed to the content of their field(s) of specialization, and they are more likely to be concerned about content questions than about methodological matters. Their initial expectations of supervisors are therefore likely to relate to *what,* rather than *how*, they are teaching. In such cases, supervisors must earn the confidence of teachers not by their demonstrated command of subject-matter knowledge, but rather by their ability to raise questions about the content, about the apparent responses of pupils to the content as presented, and about the larger setting within which the teacher, the pupils, and the content ideas are interacting.

COLLABORATION

■ As described in the literature, benefits of the collaborative approach to teacher supervision include cooperation and communication, nurturance of teacher self-confidence, reduction in teacher anxiety, and a facilitation of change in teacher behavior. Applying the collaborative model requires that supervisors adopt a style that builds trust between them and the teacher. Supervisors and administrators must be willing to accept and use a supervisory style characterized by the fundamentals of cooperation, sharing, interdependence, and harmonious interaction. Consider the contrast between the traditional role of the supervisor and the collaborative supervisory role as illustrated in Table 2.

TABLE 2

SUPERVISORY STYLES

TRADITIONAL	COLLABORATIVE
Determines the goals for teachers and methods to achieve them; interprets standards for quality and goals.	Works with teachers as they identify and resolve teaching-related problems; assists them in setting their standards.
Uses position of authority to direct the teachers, promoting a strong superior-subordinate adversary relationship.	Assists teachers in setting challenging goals for themselves by enhancing their sense of professional autonomy.
Evaluates teachers' performance as success or failure.	Educates teachers to self-examine performance; counsels them on how to learn from analysis of failures.
Develops new ways of evaluating and planning.	Induces teachers toward, and assists them in, innovative approaches.[3]

Traditionally supervisors determine goals and performance standards for teachers. In the collaborative role, supervisors participate with teachers in setting goals, thus promoting teacher self-evaluation. In all instances, supervisors must be conscious of *rapport* as a facilitating condition. Established trust will help ensure that the observation and subsequent discussions will enhance the collaborative relationship.

What is a collaborative approach to supervision? Teachers view it as a participatory approach to identifying and solving problems and issues that affect the classroom and learning outcomes of the students. Participation builds greater involvement and, hence, boosts morale. Most of the time, the real expert at identifying and solving problems connected with teaching is the person closest to the scene—the teacher. Stress the teachers' role in identifying problems: "You identify them. We'll work together in solving them."

A good system of communication, initiated and fostered by the supervisor, is the primary vehicle to building this collaborative relationship.

PEER SUPERVISION

■ In the discussion of teaming in Chapter 3, we spoke of our enthusiasm for arrangements which enable classroom teachers, as peers, to supervise each other in a collegial setting. A prerequisite, we stated, is the supportive role played by the building principal or supervisor. There is much potential in peer supervision being used in the regular classroom, especially when all teachers are properly trained.

Peer supervision is not a natural phenomenon in that CS requires much knowledge and many skills for successful implementation. Generally teachers have neither the necessary time nor expertise to act as their own supervisors or to deal competently in peer supervision without leadership which enables them to learn, develop, and maintain the requisite observational skills and knowledge base for analysis of teaching.[4] Harris cautioned that if clinical supervision relies too heavily on self-training, it may encourage over-confident attempts at change which, in the absence of needed skills, could produce failure.[5]

The early Harvard work experimented with and promulgated "team" and "peer" as integral to the CS concept and practice. Our own work with IGE at both K–12 and university levels, as well as work with individual schools and school systems corroborates the Harvard view. We see peer supervision as a strategy designed for deliberate and systematic improvement of instruction. Peer supervision, as practiced by a clinical team, provides valuable feedback and growth for both the observed teacher and the observing teacher(s). The observed teacher receives feedback on specific foci of the lesson (salient teaching patterns, student behaviors that affect learning, etc.), via data generated by a team of observers. The observer(s) in turn receives an indirect or direct better understanding of his or her own teaching by observing and analyzing others' teaching.

Many new and innovative ideas can be collected by observing someone else in the same or related field doing similar things with a teaching style different from yours. Peers generally want to do their best when their colleagues are present. Conferencing with peers about an observed lesson provides mutual exploration for improvement, opportunities to discuss alternatives, and avenues to build self-image through peer praise—for all members of the clinical team. The clinical team, consisting of several members, observes the teaching of each member. If the team has two members, the observation can be one-to-one with guidance from the supervisor. If the team has more than two members, the CS process becomes more flexible, and potentially more powerful.

Suppose, for example, the team has four members, A, B, C, and D. When observing A, members B, C, and D have designated specific roles. Member D, for example, may be a process observer, analyzing everyone's role in the clinical supervision cycle. B may be the lead supervisor, responsible for conducting the ob cycle and assigning specific roles for B and C in gathering data in the classroom observation, analyzing it afterward, and preparing a strategy for the conference. When B, C, and D are observed, respectively, roles are changed. The planned changing of roles allows more learning about and practice with the ob cycle and more learning about one's teaching. In this team process, we stress, most important is the role the clinical supervisor must play in preparing teachers to be knowledgeable and skillful in the the peer observation process. While the teaming in peer supervision process is powerful, the clinical supervisor should oversee the process and be a constantly available consultant and coordinator. When properly functioning, the peer supervision process allows CS to work more effectively with more teachers through peer teams. We feel that the success of peer supervision, and all CS, is enhanced by the understanding of and skills in the topic we address next.

MORALE

Facilitating Condition 4

The supervisor/coach and teacher must have sufficient mutual understanding of each other and of the work context. If they do, little energy is wasted on interpersonal decoding.

In all instances, but especially in cases where the supervisor must build a supervisory relationship from scratch, it is essential that the supervisor be conscious of *rapport* as a facilitating condition. (We will return to this topic momentarily.) Another important related concept guiding supervisor behavior is that one of supervision's main goals is the nurturing of healthy and confident self-concepts in teachers and, through teachers' behaviors toward pupils, in the pupils as well. Our enthusiasm for clinical supervision is fueled by our awareness that clinical approaches are particularly conducive to influencing and increasing teachers' self-respect and their healthy, positive regard for learners.

By its very nature, in-classroom observation connects supervisors to the learners, to the teacher in action, and to the various forces that impinge upon the morale and productivity of the various participants. By being one of the participants, at least to some extent, the supervisor enters into the morale picture; and every response or suggestion flowing out of that participation is a potential contribution to the ways that teachers and students feel about the content, about their relationships to it, and about themselves and each other.

Some general principles should therefore guide the supervisor toward making *positive* contributions to such feelings. Supervisors must:

- Reduce the teacher's natural tendency to be apprehensive about clinical supervision, especially since it involves a great deal of direct, face-to-face interaction.

- Enhance the teacher's sense of professional autonomy by respecting teachers for who they are and how well they do.

- Know and respect themselves so they can better respect others' ideas.
- Establish an environment to encourage initiative in teachers, respond to their creative efforts, and assist them in evaluating results of their efforts.
- Make every effort to help the teachers feel comfortable about what is being taught, deal with perceived gaps in their knowledge, and especially make certain that teachers' enthusiasm for the content is conveyed to their students.
- Be eternally conscious of the importance of maintaining rapport with teachers. This admonition is so important to us, in fact, that we want to examine rapport in more detail as an integral aspect of supervisory effectiveness.

RAPPORT

■ To be effective as a clinical supervisor, one needs knowledge built upon a foundation of theory in administration and supervision. Among the most relevant theories in these fields are those relating to the importance of motivation and of having a positive view of self. In content theories of motivation, we encourage the reader to consult the classic works of Abraham Maslow on motivation theory regarding personality, needs, and consummatory behavior;[6] of Douglas McGregor on Theories X (directed) and Y (self-directing), which represented polar assumptions about work and people[7] (McGregor's assumptions are derived from Maslow's work); of Chris Argyris on the immaturity-maturity continuum;[8] of Frederick Herzberg[9] on motivation hygiene theory; and of Rensis Likert[10] on four systems of organization.

In process theories of motivation, we encourage the reader to consult works of Leon A. Festinger[11] on cognitive dissonance theory; of J. Stacy Adams[12] on theory of social inequity; of Victor H. Vroom[13] on expectancy theory; and of Edwin A. Locke[14] on goal achievement. In behavior modification concepts, we encourage the reader to consult works of Fred Luthans and Robert Kreitner[15] on reinforcement theory. We consider these the foundational contribution to rapport.

Rapport is *a harmonious relationship with and between people*. To cultivate harmonious relationships, a clinical supervisor needs to use a knowledge base of supervision, to include elements of learning theory, motivational theory, and administration theory. To be effective, clinical supervisors must command both a knowledge of instructional theory and skill in its practical application with teachers. Throughout the process, rapport is vital. A clinical supervisor needs to know how to deal with the various anxiety feelings teachers reveal, whether conscious or unconscious. The supervisor also needs to know how to assess and then contribute toward the improvement of, the self-view (both personal and professional) of the teacher.

To do so effectively, the supervisor must first possess a healthy, positive self-concept. If you as a supervisor feel good about yourself and what you do, both as a person and as a professional (in other words, if your self-concept is healthy), you will be much better equipped to work effectively with teachers and students than if not. Without self-acceptance, no one can really work very well with other people.

Likewise the teacher cannot expect to work well with children, or expect to help them to work well with one another, if the teacher's self-acceptance and self-definition are negative. It also seems probable that relationships between people depend in part upon acceptance, even admiration, of the self-definitions that the relaters perceive in each other. If Maryanne feels good about herself with respect to a certain set of skills or characteristics, if Tony feels good about himself in similar ways, if Maryanne is pleased about the way Tony appears to feel, and Tony feels pleased about the way Maryanne appears to feel—then it would seem that Maryanne and Tony are going to feel good about their relationship.

Now, if Maryanne (the supervisor who feels good about herself) and Tony (a teacher who feels good about himself) do not know very much about each other's self-definitions, it is not as likely that a productive relationship will exist, at least for now, and an immediate need is to set various get-acquainted activities in motion. Since our postulation is that both persons are in good psychological shape (at least with respect to the roles in question) it seems likely that rapport can be developed in fairly short order. More effort will be involved if Tony has a low self-concept; and we hesitate even to deal with the effort needed if Maryanne, the supervisor, also has low self-esteem or, worse, is the one of the two with such a problem. We believe strongly that the profession cannot tolerate this type of weakness in supervisors; and in this volume the overriding assumption is that the supervisor possesses a healthy, positive self-concept. Unless this is the case, teachers will almost surely be poorly served.

We examine rapport, then, largely under the assumption that the supervisor has the personal strength necessary both to merit the confidence and respect of teachers and to cope with some of the problems and stresses that can arise when dealing with low-self-concept personnel.

Rapport is much more than just a single aspect of clinical supervision. It cannot be so limited. It is, rather, a constant throughout the process of working with people toward a given end. It is a necessary ingredient without which we cannot begin to effect improvement in schools. In essence, we envision rapport as a continual and overriding aspect of the clinical supervisory process, an ingredient required in all phases. How then can we provide a better image of supervision in the school in which rapport will characterize all interactions between supervisor and teacher?

SELF-ACCEPTANCE

■ Already established is that supervisors must know and feel good about themselves as persons and as professionals. Another need is for supervisors to understand and be committed to promoting certain school climate conditions that are believed to foster growth. Finally, supervisors need skills that enable them to connect to the teachers served in a productive way.

The Association for Supervision and Curriculum Development (ASCD) has issued many excellent publications over the years, but none has been more influential or received more acclaim than the 1962 yearbook *Perceiving, Behaving, Becoming.* Still a strong and relevant statement after several decades, the yearbook deserves attention by all persons who seek guidance about the kind of classroom climate and working relationships that must be present in order for teachers to effect a proper learning climate with students. One chapter calls for classroom climates that:

1. Encourage self-revelation rather than self-defense.
2. Give each person a feeling of belonging.
3. Create the impression that difference is good and desirable.
4. Encourage children to trust their own organisms.
5. Emphasize the existential, ongoing character of learning.
6. Are generally hopeful.[16]

Although these climate descriptions were intended to be used by teachers working with students, they can just as easily be used by supervisors working with teachers. In fact, such a climate must be present for supervisors to be able to effect changes with teachers. As the yearbook describes it:

> Teachers in service should be treated in the same way that teachers are expected to treat students. Becoming teachers are more likely to see evidence of becoming in students. Teachers should be helped to grow through accepting, understanding and assisting them in identifying problems which they feel need solution. The supervisor who is aware that teachers are in the process of becoming works in ways which help them develop a positive view of self.[17]

Some cues for supervisors seeking to establish this sort of climate may be found in the following suggestions for self-awareness and self-acceptance:

1. **Know yourself.**

   Once in a while sit down and ask yourself "Who am I? What am I?" You might also occasionally ask others those same questions about yourself. By asking others, you might even discover things about yourself that you were not previously aware of; things you probably ought to know about yourself. Asking others is, in a sense, inviting constructive criticism. Each of us is unique, a composite of values, attitudes, and experiences. If we accept this fact, we will also accept the fact that we view others both directly through our experiences and reflectively through theirs. Clinical supervisors who know themselves and are cognizant of experiences that have contributed to their present status can interact with others more openly and more professionally.

2. **Accept yourself.**

   Accept yourself for what you are; if you do not, you will find it most difficult to accept others for what they are. For clinical supervisors working with teachers, self-acceptance is paramount for establishing a trust base. Self-confidence enhances confidence in others, and the self-confident clinical supervisor can pass confidence on to teachers, who in turn can accept and encourage students.

3. **Respect yourself.**

   Self-respect is also a must for clinical supervisors. If you do not respect yourself, how can you get others to respect you? Believe in yourself; evaluate your innate abilities; diminish your weaknesses by building from your strengths; gain sufficient knowledge in all aspects of the supervisorship; keep current and active professionally; listen to ideas of others.

4. **Respect others.**

   Success in such efforts will better equip supervisors with a readiness to respect others. For teachers to gain respect from students, they must first show respect for them. Similarly, for clinical supervisors to garner the respect of the teachers with whom they work, they must first show respect. By listening to others and accepting their ideas and mannerisms we build respect, both for ourselves and for others.

RAPPORT NURTURANCE

Facilitating Condition 5

The past is prologue. Supervisor awareness of the previous supervisory episodes and teacher efforts to improve can be of enormous help. Questions and answers relating to previous help received, teacher reactions to the help/coaching provided, successes and failures, and agreements for improvement targets can provide a foundation on which a fruitful cycle can be built.

Despite the notion that "leaders are born, not made," evidence indicates that successful leaders demonstrate many similar behaviors and characteristics, all of which are learned first by their desire to obtain the behaviors, and then through their practice and experience with the behaviors. As previously stated, clinical supervisors must command both a knowledge of instructional theory and skill in its practical applications with teachers. Throughout that skill implementation, rapport is vital. Nurturing rapport calls attention to the necessity of getting off to a good start and being sure that a positive, caring, and mutually comfortable relationship exists between the teacher (or other professionals being supervised/coached) and the person who is to play the role of coach or supervisor. Nurturance means *to nourish or to promote development or growth.* Thus rapport nurturance is *the nourishing and developing of a harmonious relationship between the clinical supervisor and teachers.* The responsibility for nourishing this type of relationship belongs to the clinical supervisor. The nurturance must be a continual, conscious process. It necessitates use of human relations skills, in appropriate degrees, and with appropriate timing.

The first skill required is a genuine like, regard, and respect for people as individuals. This seems less an active type of behavior than an innate, down-deep characteristic; but without this skill, all other behaviors must come across as both artificial and superficial, and are not apt to fool anyone.

A second skill is embedded in the continued effort by the supervisor to accept the role of sharing, cooperating, and helping. Analysis of teaching and of the teacher's role requires great competency if the analyses are to provide guidance and direction. Vital to rapport nurturance, this skill includes the ability to listen without passing judgment, to demonstrate patience, to understand where the teacher is coming from, and to recognize a good job well done.

How can clinical supervisors bring about better rapport with teachers—and how can it be nurtured? Rapport nurturance should be a continuing concern for supervisors, and from time to time might well be the subject of a specific self in-service program, in connection with which we have a brief list of suggestions:

1. Examine thoroughly and then list the present types of contacts the clinical supervisor has with teachers that could either promote or injure rapport. Then choose from that list as many as ten types of contacts you believe will promote rapport and, for each of them, discuss ways to cultivate advantages of those pleasant contacts. From the original list, construct a list of types of contacts you believe injure rapport nurturance and, for each of these, discuss ways in which these contacts could be made more nurturant.

2. Examine the types of praise clinical supervision affords teachers. Then, analyze the types of praise you, as a clinical supervisor, tend to use with teachers, and how you may praise more effectively.

3. Have supervisors participate in simulation exercises designed to show the importance of both verbal and nonverbal communication.

   a. Pair two supervisors and have them read aloud to each other, in turn, a selection of names or ads from the telephone directory, as if they were: bored; exasperated; thrilled; unhappy; rushed; confiding.

   b. Pair two supervisors and have them shake hands showing the same feelings as above.

   c. Pair two supervisors and have them, in turn, use body gestures or movements and facial expressions to demonstrate the feelings above.

SUMMARY

Clinical supervision success requires a careful blending of interpersonal and technical considerations. We consider the five facilitating conditions listed in this chapter essential to setting the stage to CS.

Whether on a one-to-one basis or through a team effort, self- acceptance, morale, and rapport are integral to CS facilitating conditions. In the original Harvard model, teaming and peer observations were used successfully in the cycle. We encourage their use when possible. Rapport nurturance serves as a continual reminder of the importance of blending interpersonal and technical considerations for CS success. We encourage the reader to develop as many of the nurturance techniques as possible and use them accordingly.

REFERENCES

[1] Fred T. Wilhelms, *Supervision in a New Key,* Association for Supervision and Curriculum Development, Washington, D.C., 1973, p. 1.

[2] Morris L. Cogan, *Clinical Supervision,* Houghton Mifflin, Boston, 1973, p. 21.

[3] Kenneth J. Tewel, "Collaborative Supervision Theory Into Practice," *NASSP Bulletin* 7, April 1989, p. 76.

[4] Francis E. Bloomer & Robert J. Krajewski, "The Supervisor in IGE: A Neglected Role," *Texas Tech Journal of Education 3,* 1976, pp. 177–186.

[5] Ben M. Harris, "Limits and Supplements to Formal Clinical Procedures," *The Journal of Research and Development in Education 9,* Winter 1976, pp. 85–89.

[6] Abraham H. Maslow, *Motivation and Personality,* Harper & Row, New York, 1954.

[7] Douglas McGregor, *The Human Side of Enterprise,* McGraw-Hill, New York, 1960. See also Douglas McGregor, *Leadership and Motivation,* MIT Press, Boston, 1966.

[8] Chris Argyris, *Personality and Organization,* Harper & Row, New York, 1957; *Interpersonal Competence and Organizational Effectiveness,* Dorsey Press, Homewood, Illinois, 1962; and *Integrating the Individual and the Organization,* John Wiley & Sons, New York, 1964.

[9] Frederick Herzberg, Bernard Mausner, and Barbara Synderman, *The Motivation to Work,* John Wiley & Sons, New York, 1959; and Frederick Herzberg, *Work and The Nature of Man,* World Publishing Co., New York, 1966.

[10] Rensis Likert, *The Human Organization,* McGraw-Hill, New York, 1967; *New Patterns of Management,* McGraw-Hill, New York, 1961.

[11] Leon A. Festinger, *A Theory of Cognitive Dissonance,* Stanford University Press, Palo Alto, California, 1957.

[12] J. Stacy Adams, "Toward an Understanding of Inequity," *Journal of Abnormal and Social Psychology,* 67 #5, 1963, pp. 422–436. "Inequity in Social Exchange," in *Advances in Experimental Psychology,* ed. by L. Berkowitz, Academic Press, New York, 1966, p. 163.

[13] Victor Vroom, "Organizational Choice: A Study of Pre and Postdecision Processes," *Organizational Behavior and Human Performance,* 1966, pp. 212–225.

[14] Edwin A. Locke, "Toward a Theory of Task Motivation and Incentives," *Organizational Behavior and Human Performance 3,* 1968, pp. 157–189. Also "The Ubiquity of the Techniques of Oral Setting in Theories of and Approaches to Employee Motivation," *Academy of Management Review,* July 1978, pp. 594–601.

[15] Fred Luthans and Robert Kreitner, *Organizational Behavior Modification,* Scott Foresman, Glenview, Illinois, 1975, pp. 7–15.

[16] "Acceptance and the Accurate View of Self," *Perceiving, Behaving, Becoming: A New Focus for Education,* 1962 Yearbook, ed. by Arthur W. Combs, Association for Supervision and Curriculum Development, Washington, D.C., 1962, pp. 125 and 126.

[17] "The Process of Becoming," *Perceiving, Behaving, Becoming: A New Focus for Education,* 1962 Yearbook, ed. by Arthur W. Combs, Association for Supervision and Curriculum Development, Washington, D.C., 1962, pp. 246 and 247.

CHAPTER

5

Pre-Observation Conference

In This Chapter

- Facilitating Success
- Planning
- Guidelines
- Implementing
- Summary

Planning for the pre-observation conference is essential because how well the stage is set determines, in large measure, the success of the CS cycle. This chapter is the first of five which describes the individual stages of the cycle. It is intended to be a hands-on, practical guide to planning and implementing the pre-observation conference. It includes first a list of purposes, as viewed by both teacher and supervisor. Planning guidelines are presented, as is a practical list of problems to avoid. Finally, the key elements of the pre-observation conference are delineated and explained.

FACILITATING SUCCESS

As noted in Chapter 3, the pre-observation conference provides a mental and procedural framework for the remainder of the cycle. Its purposes include:

- Confirming and nurturing the teacher-supervisor relationship.
- Enhancing fluency in identifying the teacher's concerns and developing means to address them.
- Providing a conceptual rehearsal for lesson problem areas.
- Ensuring an agreement for rationale and method of observation.

From the *teacher's* point of view, the pre-observation conference:

- Establishes a shared decision-making climate for the entire CS cycle (and specifically the lesson to be observed).
- Identifies both long-term and more immediate teaching concerns.
- Offers time to review or to conceptually rehearse (or both) a lesson that has been planned.

From the *supervisor's* point of view, the pre-observation conference:

- Communicates the teacher's professional needs, interests, and feelings.

- Allows observation ground rules to be cooperatively determined.
- Sets the tone for the entire supervisory experience.

The obvious goal is for mutual understanding and agreement for pre-observation conference purposes and procedures, and it remains the supervisor's responsibility to effect the mutual understanding. Thus, how supervisors prepare for the pre-observation conference depends to a great degree upon what they already know about the teacher from previous interaction. How successful the supervisor is depends on the existing teacher-supervisor rapport. Above all, it is important in the pre-observation conference to continue nurturing the rapport previously established.

PLANNING

■ Planning for the conference provides both supervisors and teachers an opportunity to translate the teacher's needs and concerns into observable behaviors and to select the data gathering instruments appropriate for the next phase of the cycle, Observation. Facilitating Conditions 1 through 5, previously described in Chapter 4, might be reviewed, as appropriate in planning (and sometimes implementing) the pre-observation conference:

1. Specific, school-wide improvement goals should be in place.
2. Immediate and long-range personal teaching objectives have been defined by the teacher.
3. An agenda that targets a growth plan with timeline and progress checks has been established by the supervisor and teacher.
4. A mutual trust and understanding of concerns and perceptions of procedures for improving the teacher's instruction is established by the supervisor and teacher.
5. Successes and failures of previous supervisory episodes are discussed and evaluated.

Therefore the supervisor must approach the pre-observation conference well prepared, insofar as advance information and the teacher's supervisory history make it possible. The supervisor must comprehend exactly what the teacher intends to do and what the teacher wants the supervisor to do and, with such understanding, must function responsively. To enhance pre-observation conference success, we suggest the supervisor ask the teacher when he or she wishes to have a lesson observed and ask the teacher to provide a lesson plan prior to the conference. The plan should include answers to such questions as:

- What are the lesson objectives and outcomes?
- What teaching strategies will be used?
- What are the teacher's concerns in presenting the lesson?

The supervisor must also be sure that the arrangements made for the pre-observation conference will be convenient and comfortable for the teacher. Ideally the conference should be scheduled at a time when the teacher is free to devote full attention to it, and in a location which facilitates the trusting relationships already established.

The clinical supervisor assesses the situations and issues with an eye for the individual differences within teachers, classrooms, and students. Some guiding principles can be suggested:

- Deal in the teacher's terms and conceptual framework.
- Avoid supervisory techniques which were unsettling to the teacher in the past, or are likely to be disquieting at the moment. To illustrate, suppose the teacher expresses anxiety when inductive techniques are used to pursue a line of inquiry, or appears uncomfortable when interrogated, or is upset when compared to a peer or the supervisor.
- Try not to raise questions, offer criticisms, or make suggestions that are likely to undermine the teacher's security or strategy for the lesson at hand.
- Make special efforts to ensure that communication is clear. Statements made by either party should be probed to clarify the understanding and encourage careful consideration of the response.

GUIDELINES

■ An ideal supervisor, considering Facilitating Conditions 1 through 5 and the guiding principles offered, would do the following in the pre-observation conference:

- Formulate ideas and statements to be used.
- Hear and understand the teacher.
- Read the teacher's meanings both at face value and in symbolic terms while checking for anxiety or stress.
- Develop responses for expressions of ideas and feelings.

- Keep the range of behavior consistent with long-range and immediate supervisory goals.
- Monitor personal feelings, impulses, and motives to keep the supervisory work aimed at the teacher's improvement.

These "shoulds" represent a distillation from supervision we have researched and practiced and observed, of techniques that seemed to work, and of elements of supervision that seemed to be missing on occasions when supervision failed.

Potential Problem Situations

Even the ideal supervisor cannot ensure CS success. We can think of no better way to drive home the reality that clinical supervision is no panacea for educational reforms than by showing candidly things that can go wrong.

Problem The supervisor provides emotional support to the teacher, loses focus, and may damage or lessen the rapport established for lesson improvement.
Discussion Pre-observation is most likely to succeed if the supervisor is attentive equally to its interactional processes as potential sources of incidental learning and to the business at hand. Our insistence upon this principle is motivated as much by practical concerns as it is by philosophical ones. If the supervisor is not deliberate in self-behavior, then that behavior can easily operate at direct cross-purposes with the intended outcomes.

Problem A supervisor may upset the teacher by suggesting new elements be assimilated into the teaching plan just prior to the start of class.
Discussion Avoid introducing novelties in the pre-observation conference. Except for small, manageable refinements that the teacher can incorporate easily into the plan, new ideas, goals, and strategies are not likely to be assimilable if formulated directly before teaching is to occur.

Problem A supervisor, wanting the teacher's success too badly (and compensating for the teacher's previous deficiencies), attempts to refine the teacher's plans.
Discussion Protecting the teacher from likely problems in the existing plan by modifying the plan and disturbing the teacher's equilibrium for

that day is a delicate decision to be made. Calculating these risks is rarely simple and may result in an additional predicament, as this example illustrates:

> **SUPERVISOR:** Well, Dana, are you ready for the algebra lesson?
>
> **TEACHER:** I guess so. But I haven't quite determined how to use prepared worksheets during the lesson.
>
> **SUPERVISOR:** Earlier this morning, I just happened to reflect back on my experiences in teaching math and it occurred to me that I always made it a standard practice when using prepared worksheets to . . .

Here, the supervisor gives the teacher an answer based on personal experience, and at this stage of development as a teacher she needs probably a more indirect type of assistance—something she can work through with the supervisor with meaningful input. The supervisor has misread her asking for help, and has interfered with a more appropriate response to the teacher's problem at hand, such as "Well, Dana, what are some possibilities you considered?" This would be followed by: "Can we look at some possibilities together?" or "Do you have in mind some methods which have been successful before?"

The supervisor's own anxieties should be isolated from those of the teacher. Typically supervisors reverse the scenario, obscuring the teacher's doubts by imposing their own enthusiasm. The result: the teacher executes a lesson with serious misgivings, feeling basically insecure. The lesson is stilted and unnatural.

Problem The supervisor uses only an indirect/humanistic approach to the exclusion of all other approaches.

Discussion Helping a teacher translate concerns into observable behavior requires straight talk during pre-observation, which is one of the most productive stages of the clinical supervision sequence. For example:

> **TEACHER** *(with ten minutes left until class time)*: Just one thing—do you think it would better to send the kids to the lab tables by rows, or tell the whole class to go to their places at the same time?
>
> **SUPERVISOR:** In what ways is this a problem for you?
>
> **TEACHER:** Well, I want them to be able to get involved with the equipment right at that moment when their interest in the problem is at its height, and I'm not sure which system would be the most efficient. I guess I'll send them row by row, as fast as I can.

SUPERVISOR: Umm. Something to consider, though, is that by the time the kids in the last row get called, they may have cooled off pretty much.

TEACHER: Yeah, maybe you're right. *(Pause.)* Okay, I'll send them all at once.

SUPERVISOR: Okay, but then you have to take into consideration that if things get too noisy or out of hand and you have to stop things to discipline them, that would delay the lab work, too.

TEACHER *(glancing at his watch nervously)*: That's true. *(Long pause.)*

If supervisors are reluctant to function directly because the teacher appears to be excessively dependent upon supervision for advice and directions, we propose, nevertheless, that some relaxation of "tried and true" autonomy-building strategies can be helpful and appropriate during pre-observation.

Problem The supervisor does things that would be better done by the teacher for the teacher to benefit from the rehearsal. For example:

TEACHER: I'm not quite sure how to phrase the question so that it stimulates a lot of discussion. Do you?

SUPERVISOR: Well, I think if you ask them how it might be possible for men to build underwater dwellings, and not give them any direct hints, and not ask them whether such a thing might be possible, that should get them going on it. Let me see, uh, "How could we build . . . ?" And so on.

Discussion Supervisors should not mistakenly assume, nor should teachers, that because their own understanding of a technique is articulate and that because they have verbalized their understanding, it follows that the supervisee (or the pupil) understands it too. In this example it may be the case that supervisors' repeated attempts to frame an efficient question for the lesson will be of considerable less utility to teachers than opportunities for trying to frame their own questions would be.

Problem The supervisor tries to effect closure too soon.
Discussion Closure is not a necessary prerequisite for the pre-observation conference to be successful. In fact, many unnecessary problems result from the supervisor's desire to achieve closure. It must

be remembered that the supervision process we envision is an arduous, time-consuming process.

As clinical supervisors, our objective is teacher improvement. Improvement is not an easy task and it is not meant to be. It is not a task of short duration, nor is it meant to be. The rapport of which we speak is important to the clinical supervision process.

The pre-observation conference affords an opportunity for previous rapport nurturing to continue or improve.

- It allows supervisor and teacher to introduce and/or review their communication patterns and become more familiar with each other's interactive style.

- It allows the supervisor to use (previously suggested) rapport-nurturing promotion ideas to help eliminate, to a degree, problems of reestablishing mutual agreements toward clinical supervision.

- It allows supervisor and teacher to reduce apprehensiveness present in the CS interaction process.

We suggest therefore that a supervisor cannot risk losing rapport for the sake of reaching closure during pre-observation. There will be other opportunities for pre-observation conferences, but seldom other opportunities for regaining rapport. Once lost, rapport is most difficult to regain.

IMPLEMENTING

■ The better the teachers know their lesson intentions, both means and ends, the better the lessons can be implemented. The better the supervisor understands the intentions, the more effective the clinical supervision process can be. We suggest the following three elements (as minimum) for the pre-observation conference.

1 Establish a "Contract" or "Agreement"

Begin by reviewing the lesson plan. The plan should be brief, possibly a single page, and contain:

- One or more objectives, as appropriate, written in precise, behavioral terms.

- Procedures and teaching techniques to be followed, and time allotment for the teaching activities.

- Key pre-selected lead questions, as well as specific praise words teacher intends to use.
- Materials to be used in teaching the lesson (overhead, chalkboard, and so forth).

Next, determine the relationship of the lesson objectives to the overall learning program (unit) being implemented. *Then*, determine the relationship of the focus of activities to be observed and the manner of documentation. Three approaches to observation are possible:

1. The first is either totally teacher-initiated and drawn from perceptions of what the supervisors might look for, or supervisor-initiated, making the teacher aware of the numerous possible options for observation. The two parties then jointly select one or several approaches that appear to meet existing teacher concerns most effectively.

2. The second approach is for the supervisor to link his or her perceptions of the teacher's concern to known research, and recommend a specific data-collection focus or approach that seems best suited for resolving teacher concerns.

3. The third approach, quite different from the first two, is predetermined in cases where a teacher is attempting to perform skillfully a particular model of teaching.

Whichever approach to observation is selected, prime consideration must be given to the teacher concerned and to the opportunities for promoting his or her professional growth.

We suggest the supervisor and teacher discuss several of the teacher's specific instructional concerns, and make use of an instructional needs survey which compares those concerns with present perceived competencies. It is helpful for both teacher and supervisor to examine the teacher's present level of competence. The model we suggest on the opposite page allows the teacher to compare intended objectives with present competencies in several different ways. The comparisons lead to specific descriptions of items on which the teacher wants feedback.

INSTRUCTIONAL NEEDS SURVEY

AREA OF INSTRUCTION AND PRIORITY OF CONCERN	PERFORMANCE LEVEL			
	Do Very Well	Usually Satisfied	Sometimes Satisfied	Need Work
_____ Planning Lessons				
_____ Stating Lesson Objectives to Students				
_____ Attention to Student Responses				
_____ Variety of Feedback				
_____ Asking Questions				
_____ Using Student Ideas				
_____ Lecturing				
_____ Praising Students				
_____ Summarizing Lesson				
_____ Evaluating Students				

Directions: Rank the above areas from 1 to 10 according to your priority of concern, with 1 being your greatest concern. Place the numbers to the left of the statement in the blank provided. Also indicate your present performance level.

An instructional needs survey such as the one above can help to further narrow the focus of observation. The supervisor should:

- Demonstrate a keen interest in the teacher's plans; accept without editorial comment, or inappropriate body language, the teacher's statements and requests for help; and raise clarifying questions in a spirit of seeking better to understand, rather than to challenge. In short, the supervisor should comport himself or herself as a sympathetic fellow-professional, not as a would-be judge.
- Try at the end to summarize what has been said, referring especially to agreement(s) reached about the matters to be studied and the kind(s) of information (data) to be collected in the process.

- Try to keep the observation focus upon a few questions or concerns. It is likely to be difficult to deal with more than a few important topics in any one cycle, and a sensible limitation in the scope of the agreement will pay dividends in quality.

From the lesson plan, instructional-needs survey, and other input, the supervisor and teacher can jointly determine the several foci for observation of and feedback from the lesson. Manner of documentation becomes the next order of business. The most important way of documenting is via objective analysis. Thus, objective instrumentation selection is critical for observation data collection.

There exist countless objective instruments to document activities and interaction in the classroom. The instrument (or combination/variation of instruments) used depends on many factors, including objectives, teacher needs, supervisor knowledge and expertise, foci of observation, and type of feedback desired. Feedback on student behavior would require a task instrument, or variation thereof; feedback on teacher behavior might require a question inventory, an interaction frequency inventory, a movement inventory, or the like; feedback on both teacher and students might require combinations of the above, or various types of interaction analysis instruments. The chosen instrument(s) should be non-threatening to teachers and students, user-friendly, reliable, objective, and available. We present an in-depth explanation of several such popular instruments in Chapter 6.

It is our hope that not only do readers as supervisor trainees become as proficient as possible with the three instruments explained in Chapter 6 but also that they become motivated to learn to use other instruments that may improve their data-gathering competence.

2 Establish Specific Plans for Carrying Out the Observation

Specific plans for carrying out the observation should include the following:

- When to observe (generally as a result of the lesson plan).
- How long to observe.
- What to observe (foci and activities determined in 1 above).
- How to observe.

How to prepare the students for the observation, where the supervisor sits or stands, and whether he or she should move about the room and/or interact with students—all this will be determined in large measure by the observation foci and the instrumentation chosen to gather objective data on the foci.

3 Determine the Remaining Cycle Logistics

Remaining cycle logistics will include:

- Time and place for the follow-up conference.
- Interval behavior guidelines.
- Tentative post-observation conference format.

The supervisor should discuss with the teacher the post-observation aspects of the CS cycle. Rapport, we feel, will be further nurtured if the teacher knows:

- How the supervisor intends to analyze the data.
- What possible strategies the supervisor proposes for the conference.
- When and where the conference will be held.
- What type of interval behavior (see Chapter 8) is expected from both supervisor and teacher.
- What the general conference format will be.
- What types of decisions are to be made in the conference.
- What is expected to happen after the conference.

SUMMARY

■ No matter how well supervisors prepare for pre-observation conferences, inevitably some things may go awry. Our objectives are to nurture the teacher-supervisory relationship, enhance teacher-supervisor fluency in identifying teacher's concerns and developing means to address them, provide a conceptual rehearsal for lesson problem areas, and ensure an agreement for rationale and method of observation. Hopefully we can reach these objectives but sometimes we need to be reminded not to come on too strongly so as not to unnerve the teacher, behave in too direct a manner, or impose our priorities on the teacher.

As clinical supervisors, our objective is teacher improvement, which is seldom an easy or brief task. Rapport, ever important in the clinical supervision process, must be nurtured; a supervisor cannot risk losing rapport for the sake of obtaining objectives at any cost during pre-observation conferences. Once lost, rapport is difficult to regain and CS correspondingly difficult to achieve.

Sample Lesson Plan

Objectives (one or more, as appropriate, written in precise behavioral terms): ______________________________

____

____

____

____

Teaching Strategies to be Followed (and time allotment for the teaching activities): ______________________________

____

____

____

____

Stimulating Questions to be Asked (as well as specific praise-words teacher intends to use): ______________________________

____

____

____

____

Materials to be Used in Teaching the Lesson (such as chalkboard, overhead, and so forth, and when and how they will be used): ____________

____

____

____

____

Student Evaluation: ______________________________

____

____

____

____

Self-Evaluation: ______________________________

____

____

____

____

CHAPTER

6

OBSERVATION

In This Chapter

- Facilitating Success
- Observation Systems
- Concerns
- Summary

Sometimes labeled by the term *data gathering,* observation is the activity through which a supervisor becomes aware of the events, interactions, physical elements, and other phenomena in a particular place (classroom, laboratory, library, or elsewhere) during a particular period of time. Observation is the link between pre-observation promises made and post-observation conference promises kept to seek answers to the teacher's questions. It is what a supervisor does in order to be able to test whether answers to the teacher's questions can in fact be found. It is the effort to find out what actually happens in the situations that gives birth to the teacher's questions in the first place. This chapter provides a description of various observation instruments and explanation of observation procedures. In addition to the "what" and "how" issues of observation, it also addresses "why."

FACILITATING SUCCESS

Facilitating Condition 6

The pre-observation agreement must be respected as a contract. The supervisor's arrival, classroom location, data collection techniques, planned behavior while in the classroom, and departure should conform to agreement expectations. Don't give the teacher any surprises.

Decisions about procedure and scope will have been made jointly with the teacher in the pre-observation conference. When and how the supervisor arrives in the class and departs from the class depends on the purpose and length of the observation, the type of equipment needed (if any), the observation instrument(s) to be used, and the pre-arranged necessary communication between the supervisor and teacher. A well-designed contract or agreement reduces to manageable proportions the problem of selecting items on which to focus. Instrument(s) used to collect data, therefore, depend on the already agreed upon foci for observation. Sensibly limiting scope and focusing upon matters for which relevant data can feasibly be gathered gives the supervisor much better guidance than attempting to cover too much of the waterfront. Further, a limited scope and relevant data enhance effectiveness of the overall CS effort.

Facilitating Condition 7

The supervisor's presence should be minimally distracting to students and to the teacher. Depending upon the official role of the supervisor, the presence of that supervisor in the classroom may itself be a condition to take into account. If the supervisor happens also to be the principal, established (to that point) relationships with the teacher, on the one hand, and the students, on the other, might be either a facilitating condition, a disabling condition, or neither. Therefore, we must hope that several things will be true when the principal-supervisor is in the classroom:

1. The teacher respects and trusts the principal-supervisor and therefore has essentially positive expectations.
2. The principal-supervisor visit is not a novel or unfamiliar element in the experience of the teacher and the students.
3. The students, too, respect and trust the principal-supervisor and sense no discomfort about such presence.
4. The principal-supervisor respects the confidence placed in him or her as a helping professional and behaves accordingly.

An effective supervisor can enter a classroom, fit into the scene, and be virtually unnoticed by the class even when using audio or video equipment. The teacher may or may not want to introduce the supervisor to the class, depending on the agreement. Generally, the supervisor should refrain from intervening with the lesson content or classroom management.

Facilitating Condition 8

The supervisor's apperceptive skills and data-gathering tools should be employed at full speed. There are enormous difficulties involved when an observer seeks to collect information during a classroom visit, especially a brief one. Important things happen in the classroom every minute, and usually there are as many as 30 persons whose behaviors during each minute are potentially related to the questions being explored. There is often a very rapid flow of conversation of many sorts. There may be frequent movement within the room. Many different events may be occurring simultaneously. Sounds other than voices may be audible from time to time, and even the furniture and other artifacts within the room may be moved around while the observer is present. There are four modes of recording data: audiotape, written records/scripting, videotape, and objective instrumentation. Although they are separate modes, they need not be mutually exclusive, and later in this chapter we suggest using several together, especially video- or audiotape with instrumentation. We will briefly discuss written records, audiotape, and videotape, then spend a major portion of the chapter on observation systems.

Written Record Robert Goldhammer was fond of the verbatim, or written, record, and suggested in the first edition of this book that written data have proven to be the most useful and most wieldy of all types to clinical supervisors. He listed four advantages of the written record:

1. Teachers and supervisors can assimilate it most rapidly and most easily of all data.
2. One can generally flip back and forth among pages of notes more quickly than one can return to sections of a tape.
3. By drawing arrows, circling passages, rearranging pages, or cutting and pasting, the supervisor or teacher can juxtapose sections of material to authenticate patterns of teaching or ascertain various efforts in the teaching.
4. No procedure has "shaken down" as successfully as note-taking.

Two limiting factors, he noted, are difficulty in keeping up with the lesson, and the inability of some supervisors to observe fully what is happening around them because their eyes remain glued to their notepads.

Written notes can be a valuable resource supplement and complement to objective instruments. Some instruments provide data on sociological patterns and many other types of patterns. Yet there is always need for creativity in data acquisition. For example, a skillful supervisor can use notes, diagrams, schedules, charts, symbols, and other formats, to show that a teacher may:

- Regularly pay more attention to half of the room.
- Rarely look at children in the row next to the window.
- Ask probing questions to only certain students.
- Favor students seated up front.
- Praise some students more (perhaps much more) than others.
- Have a predictable traffic pattern.
- Use certain nonverbal patterns with certain students.
- Focus on only a few children.
- Regularly exclude some students from the lesson.
- Use only one or two praise words exclusively.

- Assist only specific children at their seats.
- Use sarcasm with certain students, and so on.

Objective instruments, though integral to effective CS, can and should be supplemented by creative note-taking.

Audiotape Now that audiotape recorders have been miniaturized and are available at very low cost, it would seem that every supervisor ought to carry at least one recorder and several tapes with him or her everywhere. Keeping it running during an observation would reduce the pressure on note-taking, because one could always fill in the gaps during replay. Being able to put the recorder in one corner while sitting in another might extend the range of collectible information. Talking into the recorder on the way down the hall, outside the building, or in the car on the way to another school could double or triple the supervisor's chances of remembering important things. Audio recording has limitations, but all the same, it is a potentially excellent resource.

Videotape When Robert Goldhammer began his work in clinical supervision, videotaping was somewhat cumbersome. The recorder/playback box required a separate camera. The equipment was not very portable. Wires seemed to be all over the place, and sometimes the microphone cord, acting as an antenna, made for creative but unintended playback. In 1971, a supervisor taped a history class in coastal North Carolina, and was shocked on playing it back to hear not the teacher's voice but a newscaster from Omaha, Nebraska. Technological progress now allows the supervisor to hold in the palm of his or her hand a cordless recorder with an internal microphone.

Videotaping is an extremely helpful resource in supervision. Often not only the supervisor but the teacher will replay the tape after a lesson, in preparation for the post-observation conference. Having the tape available during a conference also has great merit, both to verify or correct recollections and to enable additional analysis to occur. In one graduate supervision class, for example, the students went over the same lesson (on tape) in six different class sessions, each time looking at a different type of question and, in the process, discovering that even in the sixth viewing there were surprises to be found.

Krajewski has several decades of experience with using videotape and objective instruments in CS cycles from kindergarten through graduate classes. In 1969, he devised the model depicted in Figure 11 (which appears later in this chapter), used it in his action research dissertation with MAT (Master of Arts in Teaching) interns teaching in junior and senior high schools, and uses it still today. We encourage supervisors to learn how to use video to supplement and complement objective instruments. Video is as versatile as the supervisor wishes and serves as an excellent visual reinforcer; use video for capturing sequences relating to only one focus, and perhaps for a maximum of 10 to 12 minutes per classroom visit. Be cautioned, however, that video is simply an instrument, and its potential cannot exceed the skills of the supervisor using it.

OBSERVATION SYSTEMS

■ We recommend objective instrumentation to gather classroom data. More than 100 objective observation instruments whose uses include teacher training, research, supervision, and specifying the conditions of learning have been tested and used in the classroom. Many measure affective and almost as many measure cognitive criteria; still others measure psychomotor, activity, content, sociological structure, and physical environment dimensions. Categorizations within these dimensions include teacher-pupil interaction, classroom climate, talk flow, verbal analysis, use of space, skill maintenance, nonverbal communication, levels of questioning, body language, and group roles, tasks, and responsibilities. Some instruments focus on observing one or two persons at a time, but most focus on groups of three or more. Some focus on the teacher, some on the pupil, but most focus on both. Some focus on verbal behavior, some on nonverbal, and others on both. Some require only one observer, some require two or more. Some require audio- or videotape as well. Bales, Bellack, Blumberg, Flanders, Galloway, Hough, Hunter, Joyce, MacGraw, Medley, Ober, Roberson, Taba, and Withall are the developers of some of the more popular instruments from which to choose.

Because scholars have been able to identify instructional variables that correlate with learning outcomes or specific teaching models, we can now guide the observation and data collection focus toward those practices that appear to matter (e.g., time on task, instructional cues and directives, reinforcement, student participation, and correctives and feedback). Research-based observation makes sense because it not only gives teachers important messages about what makes a difference but also tends to maximize the effectiveness of supervisory observations and to result in behavior reinforcements, modifications, and alterations that may have significant impact on the learning process itself.

As discussed in a previous chapter, three approaches to observation are possible today. The first is either totally teacher-initiated, drawn from teacher perceptions of what to look for, or supervisor-initiated, making the teacher aware of the numerous possible options for observation and then jointly selecting one or several that appear to meet the teacher's concerns most effectively. The second approach is for the supervisor to link his or her perceptions of the teacher's concern to known research, and then recommend the specific data collection focus or approach that seems best suited for resolving teacher concerns. The third approach, which is quite different from the first two, is predetermined in cases where a teacher is attempting to perform skillfully a particular model of teaching.

Whichever approach to observation is selected, prime consideration must be given to the teacher concerned and to his or her professional growth.

We have discovered that, for classroom use, teachers prefer an instrument that is simple to use and interpret. They desire practical approaches, and thus prefer instruments they can eventually self-administer. We concur. We present three such instruments in this chapter: Flanders' Interaction Analysis Category (FIAC) system, Behavior-Based Observation (BBO), and a Teacher Question Index (TQI).

Wilhelms has noted: "If I had to choose just one tool with which to take the process of teaching apart to see what makes it tick—and thereby improve the process—that tool would be 'interaction analysis.'" He goes on to say: "I have a hunch that administrators and teachers have hung back from using Flanders' Interaction Analysis Category system (FIAC) largely because they think it is a terribly complex and difficult process. Such fears are unjustified."[1] FIAC is one of the simplest instruments to understand and use and has excellent practical classroom application. We suggest that it be used in conjunction with videotape and other objective means.

Flanders' Interaction Analysis Category (FIAC) System

This socio-psychological system, developed by Ned Flanders, records and measures student and teacher classroom verbal interaction into ten categories.

The first categories comprise *indirect teacher influence:*

1. Accepting feelings
2. Praising or encouraging
3. Accepting ideas
4. Asking questions

The next, *direct teacher influence:*

5. Lecturing
6. Giving directions
7. Criticizing or justifying authority

Then, *student talk:*

8. Responding
9. Initiating

Finally:

10. Silence or confusion.

To use FIAC, you must first memorize, by number, the ten observation categories. During observation, record every three seconds the category number of the observed interaction behavior in column sequence, keeping your recording tempo steady and accurate.

For example, an eighth-grade mathematics class segment might start off thus: the teacher lectures (5s), then asks a question (4); after a pause (10), the teacher rephrases the question (4), and a student answers (8). The teacher then clarifies that answer (3), writing it on the board. Students are called upon (6) at random to answer a related question—and several do (8s). The class is praised (2) and the teacher comes back with an inquiry (4) related to the students' responses. Students initiate ideas of their own (9s), resulting in a boisterous discussion which the teacher calms (7s) and redirects to the related topic, telling students the correct manner to do the problem (6 and 5s). The teacher then asks a question (4) and students give short answers (8s). Students interject ideas of their own (9s); the teacher criticizes the direction of their responses (7s), asks another question (4), and receives short replies (8s and 9). The teacher rewords responses, praises the class for attentiveness and direction of their contribution (3 and 2), summarizes the lesson (5s), and gives an assignment (6).

FIGURE 3 **FIGURE 4**

FIAC Evaluation of an Eighth-Grade Mathematics Lesson on Ratios

10	3	9	8	8
5	6	7	8	9
5	8	7	9	3
5	8	6	9	2
5	8	5	9	2
10	2	5	7	5
4	2	5	10	5
10	4	5	10	6
4	9	4	4	6
8	9	8	8	6
				10

When you record the numbers, simply write them down (Figure 3) in columns top to bottom and from the left column to the right. Now pair off the numbers as in Figure 4—first pair (10,5), second pair (5,5), third (5,5), fourth (5,5), fifth (5,10), and so forth—then tabulate these pairs in the appropriate cells of a 10 x 10 matrix (Figure 5, below). Make one matrix entry for each ordered pair of numbers listed (the first number designates row, and the second number designates column). For example, with the first ordered pair (10,5) look down to Row 10, then across to Column 5, and make an entry; with the seventh ordered pair (4,10), look down to Row 4 and across to Column 10, and make an entry. When all the entries are made, total each of the columns, 1 through 10, and also the overall total as can be observed in the matrix (Figure 5).

FIGURE 5

	1	2	3	4	5	6	7	8	9	10	TOTAL
1											
2		/ 1		/ 1	/ 1						3
3		/ 1				/ 1					2
4								/// 3	/ 1	/ 1	5
5				/ 1	///// /// 8	/ 1				/ 1	11
6					/ 1	// 2		/ 1		/ 1	5
7						/ 1	// 2			/ 1	4
8		/ 1	/ 1					///// 5	// 2		9
9			/ 1				// 2		/// 3		6
10				/// 3	/ 1					/ 1	5
TOTAL		3	2	5	11	5	4	9	6	5	50
PERCENT (%)		6	4	10	22	10	8	18	12	10	100%

TEACHER TALK
COLUMNS 1-7
60%
% OF TOTAL TALK

.6
I.D. RATIO

STUDENT TALK
COLUMNS 8-9
30%
% OF TOTAL TALK

Columns 1-7 / Columns 1-10

Columns 1-4 / Columns 1-10

Columns 8-9 / Columns 1-10

Note: This matrix shows both tallies and numbers.

For a 20-minute observation, you would enter approximately 400 tallies. For a 40-minute observation, 800. We suggest that you practice enough with FIAC so that you become proficient in it.

Questions and answers are crucial to effective teaching. When and how a teacher asks questions, when and how students respond, and how the teacher reacts to students' responses, initiations, and interactions—all these can be measured through sequential analysis of the FIAC matrix. We provide several hypothetical examples of raw analysis in Figures 6 and 7.

FIGURE 6

	1	2	3	4	5	6	7	8	9	10
4				2	1	1		26	19	3

Figure 6 indicates that the teacher asks questions well. Questions are followed mostly by answers from students called upon (Box 4–8), and by answers from students volunteering (Box 4–9). Students apparently know the answers, as evidenced by the small number of entries in Box 4–10.

FIGURE 7

	1	2	3	4	5	6	7	8	9	10
4	1		2	32	16	22	6	9	5	22

In Figure 7, the teacher either drags out questions or poses them unclearly (32 entries in Box 4–4), lectures after questioning (Box 4–5), and criticizes following questions (Box 4–7). Students either do not understand the questions or do not know the answers (as shown by the numerous entries in Box 4–10). There may be discipline problems, confusion, a lack of planning for the lesson, or all these. These examples show that we can, in row analysis, determine sequential interaction; and we can make sequential analysis as specific as we wish.

These few examples should assist you in beginning to understand the analysis process used with the matrix system. We will address FIAC again in the Analysis and Strategy chapter.

Behavior-Based Observation (BBO)

A variation of Frank MacGraw's technique of "At Task," Behavior-Based Observation is a useful technique for gathering data on individual behavior and student attentiveness. Using it requires these steps:

1. Designate a list of behaviors to be observed for this classroom situation, as determined in the pre-observation conference. Memorize the categories. A typical key might be:

   A – Engaged behavior

   B – Stalling

   C – Other productive work

   D – Out of seat

   E – Talking to others

   F – Non-productive work

2. Construct a seating chart in which each student is represented by a rectangle (see Figure 8).

3. Station yourself in the classroom so that you can see all the students.

4. Choose a time-frame (e.g., every 2 or 3 minutes), and number each such period (e.g., 1 through 10) within the rectangles, for the duration of the observation.

5. Take a "picture" of the whole class at each designated time frame, recording with the key letters the behavior of every student. (If a student is engaged in the specified task, you may want to leave a blank. After tallying only the non-engaged behaviors, you can go back later and add the A's for engaged behaviors.)

The completed Behavior-Based Observation form shown in Figure 8, the same eighth-grade math lesson used in the FIAC example, reflects ten observations of each student during the lesson. Such examples will vary with the length of the time-frame allowed for making notations during the observation.

FIGURE 8

Seating Chart for Recording Behavior-Based Data

FRONT OF CLASSROOM

Scott	Dean	Amy	Carol
1 A 6 A	1 A 6 A	1 A 6 B	1 A 6 A
2 A 7 A	2 A 7 A	2 A 7 B	2 A 7 A
3 A 8 A	3 A 8 A	3 A 8 F	3 A 8 A
4 A 9 A	4 A 9 A	4 A 9 A	4 A 9 A
5 A 10 A	5 A 10 A	5 B 10 A	5 A 10 A

Ryean	Jennifer	Kristen	Clifford
1 A 6 E	1 A 6 F	1 A 6 A	1 A 6 A
2 A 7 A	2 A 7 F	2 A 7 A	2 A 7 A
3 A 8 A	3 F 8 A	3 A 8 A	3 A 8 A
4 E 9 A	4 A 9 F	4 A 9 A	4 A 9 A
5 E 10 A	5 F 10 F	5 A 10 A	5 A 10 A

Jeff	Lynn	Eric	Denny
1 E 6 E	1 E 6 A	1 A 6 A	1 A 6 A
2 E 7 A	2 E 7 A	2 A 7 A	2 A 7 A
3 E 8 B	3 E 8 A	3 A 8 A	3 A 8 A
4 E 9 A	4 A 9 A	4 A 9 A	4 A 9 A
5 A 10 F	5 A 10 A	5 A 10 A	5 A 10 A

Jo-Anne	Angela	Karolyn	Abby
1 E 6 F	1 A 6 A	1 A 6 F	1 A 6 A
2 E 7 D	2 A 7 A	2 A 7 D	2 A 7 A
3 E 8 B	3 A 8 A	3 A 8 A	3 A 8 A
4 E 9 F	4 A 9 A	4 D 9 A	4 A 9 A
5 B 10 F	5 A 10 A	5 B 10 A	5 A 10 A

ACTIVITY CODE
A = Engaged Behavior
B = Stalling
C = Other Productive Work
D = Out of Seat
E = Talking to Others
F = Non-Productive Work

TIME-FRAME CODE	
1 = 10:30 A.M.	6 = 10:40 A.M.
2 = 10:32 A.M.	7 = 10:42 A.M.
3 = 10:34 A.M.	8 = 10:44 A.M.
4 = 10:36 A.M.	9 = 10:46 A.M.
5 = 10:38 A.M.	10 = 10:48 A.M.

Data Analysis The chart shown in Figure 9 conveniently summarizes the observations recorded from the seating chart, and illustrates the importance of Behavior-Based Observation data in CS. The teacher can quickly see how many students were engaged in each behavior category. In this example, many students were attentive during the first observations and then deviated from the task. The data focuses the teacher's attention directly on the productivity of classroom behavior. The teacher quickly sees if students are not engaged in the task, and if a problem exists that needs correction. Once the problem is diagnosed, the teacher and supervisor can work out a solution.

FIGURE 9

ACTIVITY	TIME-FRAME										SUMMARY	
	1	2	3	4	5	6	7	8	9	10	Total	Percent
A. Engaged Behavior	13	13	12	12	11	10	12	13	14	13	123	76.9%
B. Stalling	0	0	0	0	3	1	1	2	0	0	7	4.4%
C. Other Productive Work	0	0	0	0	0	0	0	0	0	0	0	0%
D. Out of Seat	0	0	0	1	0	0	2	0	0	0	3	1.9%
E. Talking to Others	3	3	3	3	1	2	0	0	0	0	15	9.3%
F. Non-Productive Work	0	0	1	0	1	3	1	1	2	3	12	7.5%

Teacher Question Index (TQI)

Asking questions may be the most important activity in which teachers engage, especially if the teacher's goal is to increase students' verbal participation. The teacher's discretion when selecting levels of questions will determine to what extent the students are mentally involved, and, for the most part, student engagement level is related to teaching effectiveness.

Cognitive Question Levels Consider the six question categories below, based on Benjamin Bloom's cognitive-level taxonomy. Each level measures what knowledge the child demonstrates, the most meaningful learning occurring at the application level and beyond in hierarchal order, synthesis being the highest. Students demonstrate ability to:

1. **Know facts.**

   Student is asked to learn specific facts or vocabulary and reiterate them in a similar form. For example: "Who can define the commutative properties of algebra that we discussed yesterday?"

2. **Comprehend.**

   Student is asked to communicate knowledge and interpret previous learning. For example: "Lynn, can you explain the importance of knowing the commutative properties of operation in our use of mathematics?"

3. **Apply.**

   Student is asked to use the learned knowledge, rules or methods in new situations. For example: "Can someone think of some activities you may practice at home that are not commutative?"

4. **Analyze.**

   Student is asked to separate an idea into its parts and perceive the interrelationship or be able to divide a complex whole into its component parts. For example: "How does the rule for multiplying by powers of 10 make sense in light of our base-10 numeration system? Now that you have read the word problem on the board, who can examine it for the math operation needed to solve the problem?"

5. **Synthesize.**

   Student is asked to combine or reorganize specific parts or elements to create a whole or new structure. For example: "Who would be able to develop a formula or rule using the data from this math problem?"

The inventory is a relatively simple instrument: Using the categories provided, the supervisor tallies by type each question asked by the teacher during a lesson. A simple chart as depicted in Figure 10 (on the following page) can be used.

Each time the teacher asks a question, the supervisor makes the appropriate tally-mark on the summary chart. The chart provides a data base for analysis of teacher *intent* versus *performance*. Initially the supervisor may use the information to provide the teacher data on what types of questions were used. Then, data could be combined with other objective data to provide a more powerful analysis.

It is possible to determine what type of behavior the teacher exhibits when asking specific question types by combining this model with FIAC analysis. In FIAC, you will remember, "asking questions" is coded as Category 4. Combining the TQI and FIAC is possible by recording with a double digit: coding 4/1 for a knowledge question, 4/2 for comprehension question, and so forth. When coding to the matrix, just code the 4. However, on the original listing of coded numbers, the supervisor can possibly identify patterns of behavior for specific questions. (For example, a teacher may have different responses to students answering knowledge, application, synthesis, and analysis questions.) Such information can be quite valuable in professional growth pursuit, and is possible only from creative use of these two objective instruments.

Also valuable is data revealing which specific question types are addressed. A teacher may, for example, be asking only lower-level cognitive

FIGURE 10

Summary of Teacher Question Index from Eighth-Grade Math Class

Teacher ____________________ Date ________

Class/Subject ________________ Time ______ to ______

Descriptive notes:

____

____

____

____

____

____

____

____

____

____

Student is asked to:

Know facts	𝍸 𝍸 𝍸 ||
Comprehend	𝍸 𝍸
Apply	||
Analyze	|||
Synthesize	|

questions in the knowledge range, and fail to challenge students or measure their understanding level for that material.

Using Several Observation Instruments

We suggest using videotape in tandem with other objective instruments; they will complement one another and provide a more potent, objective basis for observing classroom instruction than any single instrument could. As you become more proficient with objective analysis instruments and videotape, you will have no problem in doing both simultaneously.

Videotaping is extremely helpful in supervision. Often, the teacher will replay the tape after a lesson, in preparation for the post-observation conference. Having the tape available during the conference also has great merit, both to verify (or correct) recollections and to foster additional analysis. Creative use allows for analysis that is both specific and detailed.

Example 1 FIAC provides information for total and sequential analysis of the number of questions asked, what occurred after they were asked (students answered, teacher repeated question, teacher answered own question, and so forth), and what happened when and if students answered. Using the TQI at the same time provides information about the kind of questions asked. Analysis may indicate, then, that:

1. When *factual* questions were asked, students answered and the teacher replied with praise, further questions, or both.
2. Few *analytic* questions were asked, and when they were, silence ensued, broken only by the teacher answering the question. *Or,*
3. The reverse of the above may prove true for factual and analytic questions.

Example 2 Behavior-Based Observation provides information about students' behavior. By combining this with videotape, teachers can see the behavior of students, as well as review it on paper, during the conference with the supervisor. Combined with TQI and FIAC, Behavior-Based Observation data will reveal what questions were asked, to which students, with what type of result—a much more powerful analysis package.

The above two examples illustrate how several instruments can be used together. The model in Figure 11 further shows how a supervisor and teacher can use combinations. The suggested model components—objectives, FIAC analysis, Behavior-Based Observation, Teacher Question Index, videotape—can be supplemented by peer ratings, supervisor ratings, or others as needed or desired. The teacher self-improvement model begins with listing of objectives in the pre-observation conference and then deciding which instruments to use in observing the lesson. The model is designed to allow the supervisor and teacher to use any or all of the instruments in lesson observation and analysis.

FIGURE 11

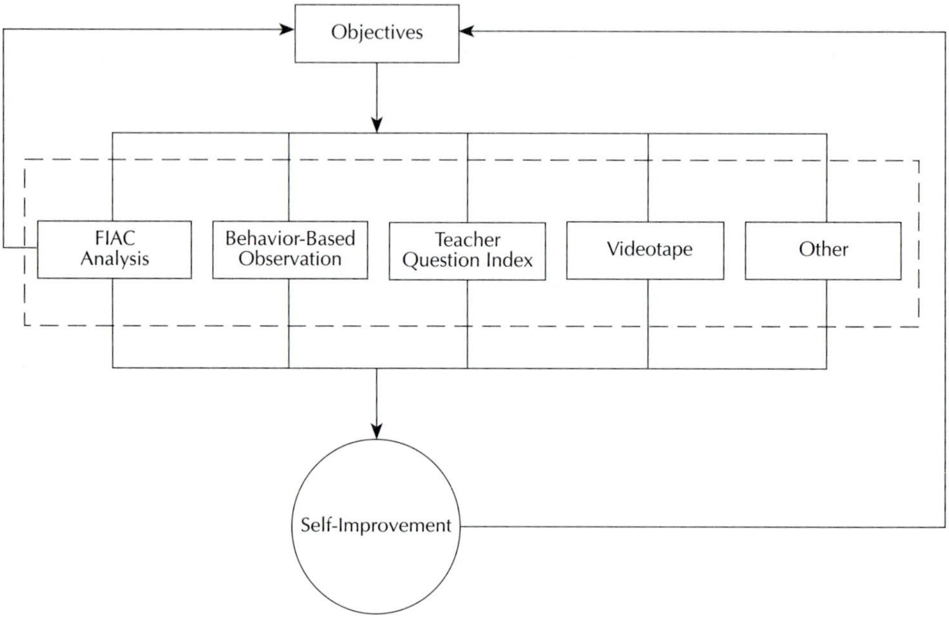

The dotted line indicates that after using one or more of these instruments the teacher and supervisor can choose to once again compare objectives. If objectives need to be changed, then the supervisor and teacher should work together to effect those changes at this time. When the supervisor and teacher reach agreement on a match of objectives and performance data from instruments, the self-improvement naturally follows. The model is cyclical and never-ending. Objectives are continually refined, then tested through the objective instruments, and analyzed. Self-improvement occurs and the cycle continues.

It would not be too difficult for teachers to eventually become proficient enough to do an FIAC in their own classrooms simply by putting a small audio recorder in the class, taping the lesson, and then just completing a Flanders' Interaction Matrix. The teachers may then, alone or in conference with the observer, progress toward objectives.

CONCERNS

■ It may be useful at this point to consider some of the difficulties supervisors encounter as they seek the right kinds of information.

The Myth of Objectivity in Data Gathering One of the most important issues to consider is that of the "objective" stance or perspective. Supervisors believe that teacher behavior data should be handled objectively—uninfluenced by emotion, surmise, personal prejudice, or bias on their part. This is a highly commendable value, and no doubt objectivity should be respected and sought in every possible way. However, it may be dangerous to assume that we have ever achieved true objectivity, and even more dangerous to base our conclusions on data because we believe them to be perfectly uncontaminated. Every time we, as observers, enter into someone else's experience, what we see and hear is inexorably filtered through our own experience, our own values, our own orientation at that moment, and the limits of our own sensory instruments.

Dangers of the Wrong Mood Supervisors, like all people, are subject to temperamental, emotional, and situational ups and downs. Perceptions, and subsequent interpretations, are inevitably influenced by the momentary mood and condition of the observer.

Problems of Physical and Psychological Distance It is a factor seldom examined that, whether in a classroom or some other observation setting, the teacher and the supervisor are, by their locations in the room, seeing and hearing two different happenings. Perhaps an even more important variable may be *emotional* distance. It is highly desirable for the supervisor to display involvement in the teacher's work. Yet, at the same time, supervisors need to be free of emotional restraints when they seek to analyze, with as much objectivity as possible, what has been observed.

Assessing the Effect of the Supervisor's Presence It is an age-old question how to take into account, when determining the success or failure of a lesson, the supervisor's presence. We think that most pupils, especially those for whom visitors are not a rarity, tend to adjust quickly. If the teacher's behavior appears calm and "normal" to the children, such tuning out is virtually guaranteed. The challenge, then, is for the supervisor to establish that supervision is a helping enterprise and that no threat is intended. When a visit appears to trigger anxiety, we suggest a graceful withdrawal, followed by some rapport-nurturing activities before the next visit.

Being Equal to the Task Some form of process or self-awareness training or counseling—that is, some set of experiences that enhance supervisors' self-knowledge, their capacity for self-monitoring, and their ability to teach teachers these same capabilities—may be a helpful supplement to supervisor training along the way. Similarly, data-gathering and observation skills ought to be continually updated and strengthened. In fact, supervisors, perhaps more than any other education professionals, need to be continual and determined students of their craft. Through such activities, supervisors can provide for their teachers an appropriate model of the true professional.

SUMMARY

To have effective data for feedback conferences, the supervisor needs a range of observation systems and recording devices. A number of such instruments were described in this chapter, most simple to understand and easy to use after a little practice. The information they provide to the teacher and supervisor are fundamental to a successful clinical cycle.

It is essential to effective observation that the understandings reached in the pre-observation discussion be respected and honored, that the supervisor be as inconspicuous and unintrusive as possible, and that every opportunity for perceiving and recording classroom events be capitalized upon.

REFERENCES

[1] Fred T. Wilhelms, *Supervision in a New Key*, ASCD, Washington, D.C., 1973, pp. 13 and 16.

ADDITIONAL REFERENCES

M. Dunkin and B. Biddle, *The Study of Teaching*, Holt, Rinehart, and Winston, Boston, 1974.

C.M. Evertson and J.L. Green, "Observation as Inquiry and Method," in *The Handbook of Research on Teaching*, 3rd ed., ed. by M.C. Wittrock, Macmillan, New York, 1986, pp. 162–213.

B. Rosenshine and N. Furst, "The Use of Direct Observation to Study Teaching," in *The Handbook of Research on Teaching*, 2nd ed., ed. by R.M.W. Traver, Rand McNally, Chicago, 1973, pp. 122–183.

A. Simon and E.G. Boyer, eds., *Mirrors for Behavior: An Anthology of Classroom Observation Instruments*, Research for Better Schools, Philadelphia, 1970 [ERIC edition 032 613].

G. Weade and C.M. Evertson, "On What Can Be Learned by Observing Teaching," *Theory into Practice 30*, Winter 1991, pp. 37–45.

CHAPTER

7

ANALYSIS AND STRATEGY

In This Chapter

- Facilitating Success
- Analysis Methods
- Strategy Methods
- Summary

Because of Dr. Goldhammer's background as a psychologist, and his intense emotional commitment to a highly professional definition of both teaching and supervision, the first edition of this book was a very intellectual, emotional, and challenging volume. This was especially true in the chapters on analysis and strategy. We toned down the second edition somewhat, almost eliminating the emotional elements. In this edition, we present analysis and strategy in a more practical framework.

FACILITATING SUCCESS

■ The main analysis ideas Robert Goldhammer valued were *saliency*, *treatability*, and *selectivity*. (Previous editions of this book used, for the last of these ideas, the somewhat ambiguous term *fewness*. We replace it here with *selectivity* in the hope that this term is clearer and more precise.) In Dr. Goldhammer's view, *saliency* meant significance and importance. He made the point that sometimes supervision does not progress beyond the incidentals of classroom functions into the things that matter most in the lives of children and teachers. By *treatability*, he meant that we need to concentrate on things about which something can be done. What he meant by *selectivity* was that one ought not deal with too much at once, being careful to choose only a few things on which both the supervisor and the teacher can concentrate manageably. So, in effect, *feasibility* is a word that we might also now include in the analysis discussion. We respect and salute Dr. Goldhammer for having introduced these major concepts into our thinking.

In lesson analysis, you begin to formulate some initial impressions of the kind of patterns characterizing a teacher's work. If this is one in a sequence of such observations, think back to what you observed in previous observations to see whether certain ways of dealing with problems or of talking or reacting to the students or moving around represents a persistent pattern, the recognition of which might be useful to the teacher. You have to review video, FIAC, charts, and graphs, and then sort it all out and sum it up: This is in fact what happened in the lesson; this is how the data relates to what the teacher hoped or predicted would happen; these are the discrepancies; this is where the teacher apparently failed;

this is where the objectives and lesson meshed and the teacher succeeded; these are the problems that came up along the way. So now the picture is more complete. Now you can say which of these data are salient, which are treatable, and then pick out a manageable number—a few of these things—to address. Then move into a strategy for addressing the treatable issues and say, "Okay, this is what I think this teacher needs to understand; these are the data I need to present to the teacher to help reinforce that understanding. How can I best go about it? How much of the data should I present in this conference? How much of it should I set aside until a later date, when the teacher may be more ready or more able to handle it?"

CS at all stages calls for a mixture of knowledge, experience, intellectuality, and communication talents. It is in the challenging analysis and strategy stage, however, where cognitive skills are most necessary. Analysis and strategy is the time to:

- Reconstruct the events observed.
- Sort and relate those events to the questions being examined.
- Analyze the noteworthy patterns and configurations of the teacher's behavior in those events.
- Consider data and interpretations that enable the teacher's questions to be addressed.
- Plan a strategy for the conference. *And,*
- Look ahead to future teacher growth and improvement.

Facilitating Condition 9

Postpone judgments, opinions, and conclusions until an objective basis has been established from thorough review of the data. Avoid labeling, and leave room for further data to influence an interpretation. Quick verdicts are hazardous and could lead to unfortunate consequences. A good question to keep asking is, "Do I now have all of the information organized and digested, so that a conclusion is warranted?"

If, for example, the teacher wants help in understanding and dealing with several specific children, then organize and study the data about those children and their responses to the teacher's actions. If the teacher is concerned about time-on-task, assemble and review data related to task engagement or non-engagement. If the stimulation of higher-level cognition is the teacher's ambition, study the data concerning student statements, questions, and speculations. We encourage the reader to refer again to the discussion of objective instruments in Chapter 6.

Ultimately, the legitimacy of any statement or question about the teacher's lesson will depend not only on careful analysis of what took place, but also the definitions of pedagogical excellence to which the involved professionals subscribe. Sergiovanni and Starratt stress that supervisors need to know their own basic opinions, beliefs, values and principles—their educational platform—from which they work. Without sufficient clarity about the supervisors' own beliefs, they suggest, it will be difficult to assist teachers in clarifying their beliefs. Thus, the purpose and preferred process of supervision; the images of supervisor, teacher, and learner and their relationships to one another; and the preferred kind of pedagogy—all these should be clearly defined and articulated items of the supervisor's educational platform.[1]

Although most teachers don't spend much time thinking or talking about the value systems and philosophical assumptions that guide their behavior, every teacher holds beliefs or convictions (for example, about children's curiosity and how to deal with it, or about fear of failure as a motivating mechanism) that prompt the use or non-use of available teaching approaches.

We perceive that by stimulating professional dialogue the CS cycle offers many opportunities for probing teachers' feelings and causing them to reexamine some of the things they feel or believe.

ANALYSIS METHODS

■ Human behavior is patterned; as a subset of general behavior, teaching is also patterned. If it is true that certain patterns of any teacher's behavior are repetitious, then it follows that the cumulative effects of such patterns are more likely to affect students' learning than occasional, isolated elements of teaching.

A teacher's unique identity has special significance. We know a person's quintessential self principally by salient behavioral patterns manifested: *Who the teacher is inevitably makes differences in how and what students learn, because the teacher's values and perceptions infuse whatever he or she teaches. Who the teacher is (and who the learners are) determines what incidental learning will be established.* In relation to both intended curricular outcomes and unintended learning that may directly affect conditions of learning, the teacher's salient patterns of behavior count more than anything else about him or her. For supervision to affect students' lives, it must be aimed at strengthening, modifying, or extinguishing these patterns. This is not easy to do because salient behavior characteristics:

- are more likely to resist change than superficial ones,
- seem to be useful to the teacher, and
- are generally reinforced by the students.

To organize data meaningfully the supervisor can formulate categories of teaching behavior:

1. Condense data to an accurate, economical representation of the teaching. Most objective instruments do this well, especially the three described in Chapter 6.

2. Search the data for authentic, repetitious behavioral patterns.

3. Document a pattern empirically before broaching it with the teacher, even if it takes more than one sequence of supervision.

4. Choose patterns whose consequences are demonstrable in the data. Most objective instruments do this well, especially the three described in Chapter 6.

One means for deciding whether data patterns are significant is to logically fit them into general categories of teaching. For example, if the teacher continually asks many-pronged questions, one could see *questioning* as the relevant category and *multiple questioning* as one of this teacher's salient patterns.

Some teachers frame their multiple questions consistently in the first person (a pattern of egocentrism) so that the implicit reason for the pupils to address the question(s) in the first place is for the teacher's sake. ("I want you to tell me how this list of numbers is ordered. Can you name the first five for me? Can you tell me the product of the last two numbers? Why is six the first number in this list? I want you to tell me the difference between this list and the one we studied yesterday.") Both the TQI and FIAC, supplemented by written records or videotape, or both, could provide data for analysis.

Another pattern is teacher-student verbalization by amount and involvement. The teacher may, for example, talk far more than the students, interact with only certain students, praise only a few students (or some more than others), or use only certain praise words (such as "okay" or "good") repeatedly. The teacher may impose his or her own value judgments upon students by including or omitting information, by distorting facts, and perhaps even by communicating incorrect information. Both FIAC and BBO, supplemented by written records or videotape, or both, could provide data for analysis.

The teacher may make promises and not keep them. The teacher may use specialized terminology inconsistently (e.g., "minus numbers" versus "negative numbers," "lines" versus "line segments"). The teacher's meanings may not always correspond with those of the students, even though conversation proceeds for a time as if there were mutual understanding. For example, a teacher may use the word "independence" in a context meaning audacious, insubordinate behavior, while the student construes independence to be a virtue, as in the "Declaration of." Or the teacher writes the example *313 x 313* on the board, and asks while trying to explain it, "And what do we do now with the three?" It may become clear that although the student's answer was correct, he was referring to a different three and, consequently, the teacher's rebuff was confusing and seemed unfair. Videotape and written records could provide data for analysis.

Sometimes the supervisor finds that the teacher tends to conduct private communications publicly or, antithetically, makes public communications privately (for example, telling Lena that the harmony exercise should both begin and end with a tonic chord, when that information logically should have been directed toward the entire class). In the process of teaching grammar, the teacher may commit precisely the errors against which he or she is cautioning ("I'm gonna do that, but we doin' somethin' else now"). Or, on the positive side, it may become apparent that while teaching about inductive reasoning, the teacher is exemplifying such reasoning in his or her own behavior. Again, videotape and written records could provide data for analysis.

In short, by reading the data and asking the question, "What is happening at this point?" sequences of behavior become apparent. The supervisor makes tentative inferences about the sequences, finds out whether the behaviors in question constitute salient patterns in the teaching, reviews inferences, tests them against data and theory, and finds which are supportable and which are not. The supervisor assembles a collection of patterns and issues, which he or she must sort out to develop strategies for the supervision conference. Having found what can be found, as in the examples above, the supervisor next attempts consciously to understand their implications and to deal with them within the values framework and pedagogical assumptions that guide his or her own supervisory behavior and goals.

A challenging problem is how to take into account the children's frame of reference as one basis for deciding which teaching behavior patterns are likely or unlikely to be salient. Try to imagine that behavior's impact upon a child in the class, and what effects might result if that behavior is enacted throughout the year. Over a long period, with the supervisor's help, the teacher's hypotheses about student response will become more accurate and useful.

Most of the time, the principal criterion for evaluating patterns is whether they helped the teacher to get what he or she was after. Allowing for goals that must sometimes be reformulated as a lesson proceeds, and taking into account that any lesson may have both long- and short-term objectives, the question can be sharpened: Does the evidence suggest that this pattern helped the teacher to get what he or she wanted at the moment(s) it was manifested? Irrespective of the teacher's prior objectives, do the pattern outcomes, particularly the incidental learnings, seem generally worthwhile or not?

After identifying patterns in the data, visually and by analysis of the substantive content, and attempting to determine their significance by reference to the teacher's goals and to the students' demonstrated or inferred experiences, the final step in analysis is to discover whether the documented patterns can be arranged in some hierarchical order. Some teaching patterns will be more prominent than others. Some patterns will seem more consequential than others—if not in relation to their frequency, then because of the likelihood that they affect particularly important areas of the students' learning and development (for example, the degree to which they accept and value themselves).

Some patterns will seem to have special importance because of their superordinate relationships to other patterns. For example, if the teacher initiates all questions and directions (category: "origins"), performs all evaluations of the students' academic progress, conducts classes so that students never have opportunities to converse with one another, and displays a prominent "I" pattern, then "teacher-centeredness," or "egocentrism," might logically be established as the superordinate pattern in reference to which all other patterns acquire special significance. "Centeredness" may be placed at the top of the hierarchy and may be employed as the organizing principle of the analysis and, subsequently, of the supervision.

Analysis problems relate primarily to categorization (how to locate and describe information), evaluation (what sense to make of perceived phenomena), and inclusion (what data to include, in the course of reviewing what took place). An observation, skillfully recorded, can produce an overload of material to be processed. Some of the data, being unrelated to the agreed-upon concerns, must be stored away or even scrapped if the cycle is not to get out of control.

Our analysis suggestions can be summarized briefly:

1. Begin analysis by reviewing the pre-observation conference agreement.
2. Arrange the data, watch for possible connections, seek to quantify and describe rather than appraise, and write down questions. Guard against subjective, premature conclusions.
3. Put data in usable, understandable, communicable form.
4. Select patterns via saliency, treatability, selectivity, and feasibility.

STRATEGY METHODS

■ Whenever two persons are scheduled to confer under circumstances where one has an advantage in information, plus the opportunity to select from that information as conscience and skill allow, the other will almost always feel somewhat at risk. Even in the best of coaching relationships, marked by mutual trust and high motivation to achieve professional excellence, there can be a degree of apprehension on the part of both persons when a feedback session is imminent. Preparing for the conference is therefore an important and sensitive activity.

The term *strategy* has become an acceptable label for planning a course of action in situations where the possible plans and reactions of other persons must be taken into account. We use the term for the thinking that goes on within the CS cycle after data have been analyzed and the coach or supervisor decides how to behave during the scheduled post-observation conference. In short, strategy incorporates decisions relating to means and ends, presently and for the future.

Ernest Steck, of Western Michigan University, is credited with the insightful remark that supervision is essentially a *word-picking exercise.* Extended to include all the gestures, intonations, body movements, and other dimensions of communication that accompany language, this is a very useful idea for supervisors to keep in mind. Whenever one has visited a teacher's classroom, especially within the context of an observation cycle, the next contact one has with that teacher is inescapably loaded with expectations and questions on the teacher's part, and every word and gesture will be weighed with great care. "How did the supervisor feel about what happened? Does he think I accomplished the goals I had in mind? Was he shocked by what I said to Sandra? Why did he seem so displeased when he walked out?" These are only a few examples of what might be on the teacher's mind.

Having analyzed and isolated various patterns of teaching behavior from the objective data, the supervisor must decide which issues to select for the conference. This means, in effect, that goals must be set in relation to which he or she can formulate selection criteria. Supervisory goals are generally conceptualized in a multidimensional framework—that is, in the context of issues and problems deriving from several overlapping frames of reference.

- Some goals are generated by the data. Take leads from features of the teaching that stand out, and from patterns of teaching which seem to carry special significance as one analyzes observational data.

- Define goals in light of continuing problems on which the supervisor and teacher have been working. It is no more correct to begin with goals than to begin with data; indeed, avoid adopting either approach exclusively.

- Conceptualize some sequence of problems that should represent a long-range design for supervision.

- Emphasize the long-term goal that teachers learn to analyze their own work.

We have already stressed that a thorough analysis must have been made and strategy goals established, and that great care is needed to insure successful delivery of whatever news or advice is on top. We now offer some thoughts about how to proceed.

- Remember that the teacher has phrased the question or concerns to be examined, and will expect the conference to focus on those matters. A safe and generally effective way to begin the conference is to review the components of the agreement, including the several selected foci, the data-gathering procedure used in observation, and whatever else may have been promised or predicted. Whether or not this strategy is selected, the supervisor or coach should think carefully about what he or she intends to say in the opening minutes of the conversation.

- Have a plan for presenting whatever statistics, descriptions, pictures, or other evidence that might be offered in support of what will be said about the observed teaching.

- Try to anticipate the teacher's reaction to these materials, and try to have ready some thoughts or data to make an awkward moment less difficult, or a happy moment more satisfying.

- Think about the time, place, and the probable physical or psychological atmosphere of the impending conference, and anticipate how this might affect the professional interchange.

- Above all, be sure that what you have planned to share with the teacher will deal in some significant way with matters of importance to him or her and to the total school community. This advice also applies to the pre-observation conference, since agreement on a trivial agenda at that conference would be regrettable. Yet even relatively low-level questions can be beefed up as a cycle proceeds, and in the analysis and strategy stage there is opportunity for the supervisor to raise the focus to a higher plane.

In general, three principles serve as selection criteria for material to be addressed in supervision: The teaching patterns (and associated issues) discussed should be salient, few in number, and—as well as can be judged beforehand—intellectually and emotionally accessible to the teacher for analysis and treatment. Before dealing directly with specific techniques employing these criteria, let us describe the clinical supervisor's reasons for adopting them.

Reasons for Saliency First, it has been argued that salient patterns will probably have the greatest effect on students' learning. Secondly, even though there may sometimes be discomfort associated with treatment of prominent teaching patterns, the teacher's confidence in, incentives for, and rewards from supervision are likely to pale if he or she perceives that supervision is merely a quibble, a string of equivocations, an obsession with superficialities. The teacher's morale will depreciate if supervision merely wastes his or her time. For supervision to seem important and be important, it must deal with issues that are important, and salient features of the teaching are more likely to satisfy this condition than peripheral ones.

Thirdly, it is generally easier to establish the significance of ancillary patterns by reference to salient patterns than vice versa. Prominent patterns of teaching can more readily serve as organizing principles for the data than can lesser elements. Fourthly, the teacher can generally recognize salient patterns in his or her own behavior more easily than superficial ones, partly because they express more of his or her style and partly because, by definition, more data are available to document such patterns. Although one occasionally encounters defensive flights into superficiality or a teacher's apparent inability to recognize prominent regularities of his or her own behavior, such cases are exceptions, or reflect the supervisor's failure to accurately predict treatability. (We will deal with this subject later.)

Reasons for Selectivity It is a common error to saturate supervision conferences with so many issues of such great significance that not even the spongiest teacher could be expected to assimilate them all. Few is usually better than many. First, the time available for any supervision conference is finite, although such conferences occasionally seem endless. Secondly, even given infinite time, the teacher does not have infinite patience or an infinite capacity for assimilating ideas or generating them. Anyhow, assimilation is only an intermediate goal at best: The real goal is to develop reasons, strategies, and techniques for working on the patterns considered—something considerably more difficult and complex than simply recognizing their existence. Concentrating on one or two foci keep the supervision process manageable and on target.

Reasons for Treatability We suspect that reasons for this criterion are self-evident. Even after supervision has become an old shoe, the supervisor sometimes guesses wrong about the psychological accessibility of certain issues and, by persevering in their treatment, generally winds up, at best, having wasted the conference time. At worst, if this sort of thing happens repeatedly, the teacher may reject supervision altogether.

Earlier in the chapter, we noted that saliency, treatability, and selectivity were the key analysis issues. We say the same for strategy. Success in implementing strategy depends on how we treat these three issues.

Saliency

How can the supervisor determine whether any given pattern of teaching is salient? What referents are germane?

The most easily satisfied condition for saliency is probably that the pattern in question should appear frequently in the teaching. But frequency alone is not a sufficient condition for establishing saliency for supervisory purposes. If it happened, for example, that every time a student responded to the teacher's questions or statements, the teacher gently scratched his ear, ear-scratching, despite its frequency, would not be worth troubling with in supervision. Frequency must be joined with *significance* to establish a useful definition of saliency. One might, in fact, attribute saliency to a pattern because of the clarity of its demonstrable effects upon the student, irrespective of its frequency in the teaching.

As suggested in our earlier discussion of analysis, some teaching patterns will seem to be highly important, even when their effect upon the children is not directly demonstrable. They might, for example, seem very appropriate—or completely inappropriate—to the children's levels of cognitive functioning. The point is that the supervisor may justifiably elect to deal with some pattern of teaching because it seems to be salient in relation to theory. Learning theory, developmental theories, and personality theories serve us most commonly in this connection. Should many teaching patterns seem to have theoretical saliency, then frequency might be taken as the determining factor for selection.

Some patterns derive saliency from their relationships to other patterns. It sometimes occurs that although analysis has unearthed a dozen patterns and although each such pattern may seem significant enough to warrant treatment in supervision, some single pattern or pair of patterns occupies a superordinate relationship to the others. Under such circumstances, the supervisor may select that single pattern that most thoroughly expresses the other's significance and may choose to grade saliency in this matter. Once a "super-pattern" has been examined in the supervision conference, it is often possible to introduce its subordinate patterns rapidly, as examples, and without elaborate analysis.

Another sense of saliency is represented by an instance in which, although the teacher manifested many inherently strong teaching patterns (call them B, C, and D), their potential effectiveness was lost because of weaknesses in architectonic pattern A. For example, one teacher's initial directions were ambiguous (category: "direction-giving"; pattern: "ambiguous"). Yet once the children had been set to work, her manner of circulating among them, welcoming their questions, and rendering individual assistance was exemplary. It might nevertheless be demonstrable that the degree to which individual students required clarifications, and the necessary repetition ensuing, betrayed the initial weakness.

Similarly, saliency might be attributed to patterns resulting in broken sequences—missing links that undermine an otherwise successful lesson.

One teacher's directions were perfectly clear, the children's tasks were clearly defined and seemed acceptable to them, and the teaching incorporated many other virtues, but at certain critical moments the lesson broke down because, when the time came to use laboratory equipment, the children did not know which apparatus to select and also found that there was not enough material to go around. The teacher's failure to muster appropriate equipment beforehand (a pattern of "failure to provide appropriate materials" or "failure to identify relevant items of equipment" or "failure to prepare the children beforehand to deal with ambiguities and shortages") might justifiably be considered salient and be isolated for supervision. In short, saliency can sometimes be defined in relationship to weak keystones or missing pieces in otherwise cogent structures.

Saliency may also be construed in normative terms—in relation to commonalities among teachers. In a departmentalized secondary school, for example, in which children are instructed by many teachers in a normal day, certain teaching patterns that do not seem particularly significant in the context of any one teacher's performance may nevertheless acquire a collective saliency that (we hypothesize) has important cumulative effects upon the students. Should it become apparent that all teachers, B through Z, employ didactic instructional approaches in which all questions and directions are formulated for the students, and should it occur that teacher A manifests this same tendency, then, in view of the children's total experience under such teaching, the supervisor might justifiably elect to address these patterns in A's teaching (or in anyone else's). Whereas a varied diet of instructional methodology might easily provide for such teaching in certain instances, an unvaried regimen of didactic teaching would fail to provide important intellectual opportunities for the students. Saliency, therefore, may be related to the surrounding scholastic environment and may be situationally determined.

Saliency may be defined in relation to what the teacher feels is important. Specific problems or teaching patterns that have been isolated in earlier supervision and upon which the teacher is deliberately working, or categories of teaching in relation to which the teacher has expressed special concern during pre-observation, can generally be placed at the top of the list of things to be considered in supervision. Relevant patterns disclosed by analysis automatically achieve a status of saliency. This is one sense of what is meant by a "teacher's frame of reference."

This method can be adopted in simple or in complex strategies. In the simplest manner, the supervisor may select patterns for the conference that the teacher has named in advance ("I want you to keep track of my verbal rewards to the children"). The supervisor detaches reward patterns from the data and examines them with the teacher in the conference. In a somewhat more complex strategy, the supervisor may decide that certain patterns are salient, not so much because the teacher has named them explicitly beforehand but rather because he suspects that there are significant relationships between such patterns and special problems in which the teacher is interested.

Using the same example, if the teacher's rewards happen to be highly responsive to idiosyncracies among the children's behavior, and if, in other dimensions of her teaching, the teacher also displays great sensitivity to individual differences (for example, in the problems she assigns, the assignments she makes, and the questions she asks), the supervisor might reasonably cite patterns of questioning, assignment-giving, and the like in order to demonstrate that in addition to mastering "good" reward patterns, the teacher's teaching, overall, constitutes a composite of patterns in which responsive behavior is pervasive. Or, to use a negative example, if the teacher's rewards are stereotyped, and if stereotypy is also evident in other categories of her teaching, then patterns belonging to such categories could be cited along with reward patterns in order to identify the broader phenomenon.

In summary, some methods for selecting patterns on a criterion of saliency are to examine them in connection with:

- Frequency and abundance in the data.
- Existence of demonstrable effects upon the students.
- Theoretical significance.
- Structural importance in the lesson.
- Commonality among teachers. *And*,
- Known or predictable significance in the teacher's already existing professional frame of reference.

Accessibility of Patterns for Treatment

There are certain complexities that inhere in clinical supervisory practice, and it is important to acknowledge them. We begin with a list of *Don'ts*:

1. *Don't* underestimate—or fail to estimate—the emotional significance of supervisory behavior for the teacher.
2. *Don't* overwhelm teachers with overly elaborate displays of data or complicated analyses filled with jargon.
3. *Don't* be reluctant to deal directly with issues.
4. *Don't* tell the teacher what is wrong and right in his or her teaching and what to do about it.

5. *Don't* focus upon specific technical elements of the teaching performance.

6. *Don't* succumb to defensive behavior. For example:

   - The teacher agrees with everything the supervisor says. In fact, the teacher agrees so readily that is possible to turn the teacher about through diametrically opposed positions.

   - The teacher consistently disagrees with almost everything and continually attributes problems to the supervisor.

   - The teacher throws up a verbal barrage, talking so much about so many things that there is little time to address specific problems thoroughly.

   - The teacher introduces red herrings: problems that seem urgent but which, because they are always outside the teacher's own behavior, effectively preclude supervision of salient teaching behavior.

Likewise, accessibility implies a number of *Do's* every supervisor should consider:

1. *Do* resist stereotyping leading to the same expectations of all teachers who display similar behavioral patterns.

2. *Do* develop some special capacity for sensing discomfort.

3. *Do* know what kinds of experiences have spelled success for the teacher previously.

4. *Do* recognize teaching patterns whose examination would probably contribute to the teacher's real and experienced success.

5. *Do* get to know the teachers and how they are likely to be affected by various approaches.

6. *Do* be flexible.

7. *Do* determine whether specific issues are accessible for treatment or not. We suggest you treat what the teacher wants to treat, and avoid what the teacher wants to avoid.

8. *Do* try to predict whether any given pattern is likely to seem essentially technical or essentially personal in the teacher's reference.

Selectivity

The following principles of selection may be useful. Any number of hierarchical arrangements are possible among these.

The Principle of Data If the supervisor has clearer or more abundant data to document some patterns than other, select those patterns for treatment, all other things being equal.

The Principle of Subsumption The supervisor may select those patterns (Class I) that subsume other patterns (Class II) either in the sense that Class II patterns represent behavioral components of Class I patterns or in the sense that the presumed significance of the latter class is incorporated by the broader significance of the former. On some occasions, this method can be reversed—namely, when the supervisor's strategy is to build from small pieces to large mosaics—that is, from patterns of lesser significance toward a synthesis of relatively greater significance. The basic reasoning for such an approach could be that the teacher is more likely to accept the existence of small, specific elements of his behavior than that of large, pervasive characteristics. Or the teacher might, predictably, feel less overwhelmed or threatened by examination of small parts than by that of large ones. Subsumptive relationships, in other words, can be used in either direction.

The Principle of Sameness or Difference For any given supervision conference, the supervisor may select patterns relating to some common category of teaching (for example, all patterns concerning classroom logistics) or may deliberately select patterns from different categories (for example, logistics, questioning, and rewards). Sameness may be desirable if the supervisor wants to develop a concentrated focus on some single dimension of the teacher's behavior. Difference may be desirable if the supervisor wants, deliberately, to broaden the base of discussion or to prevent an overemphasis of supervision in any specific category.

Sometimes it seems best to keep things open. Sometimes it seems best to home in, microscopically, with the sharpest possible degree of resolution. Sometimes the teacher needs relief, and gets it by shifting about from one set of problems to another. Sometimes the teacher feels disoriented or frustrated by such shifting and prefers to deal with one thing at a time, until he or she feels mastery in its connection. Sometimes the teacher functions best when choices have to be made. At other times he or she feels best not to be bothered by choices. Sometimes specific patterns achieve special clarity when they are treated together with related patterns. Sometimes problems become individually clearer when they are treated concurrently with very different problems.

Decisions of this order must generally be altered from teacher to teacher and in the teacher's supervision from time to time. Even though one cannot prescribe, categorically, either sameness or difference as a better principle of selection, the principle itself, used flexibly, is a very handy one.

The Principle of Loading Depending on the teacher, patterns may be selected or rejected either because of their predicted emotional loading or in spite of it. It is usually best to avoid treating anything that seems likely to make the teacher very anxious. Sometimes—especially when there are strong reasons for predicting successful outcomes—one can deliberately open an emotion-laden issue because the teacher seems right on the verge of resolving it and just ready to reap some reward. If it seems that such loading would interfere with technical progress, reject the pattern in question. If the opposite seems likely, include it. The supervisor's problem is not so much to eschew strong feelings as it is to recognize when emotionality can serve the teacher's interests in supervision and when it is likely to operate against them.

In any event, although such generalizations are never completely valid, one intuits a relationship between loading and fewness, namely, that fewness may not accomplish its objective—the purpose is to avoid saturation—if each of the few patterns selected is fraught with stressful feeling for the teacher. After patterns have been screened on saliency and accessibility, good or bad decisions on fewness can tell the story. Emotionally significant issues that might have been treated productively can be irretrievably lost if they are lumped together in the same conference in too great a number or in an infelicitous sequence.

The Principle of Time The supervisor should have a reasonable idea of how long it will take to treat specific patterns in the conference. Questions to be considered in determining the amount of time that should be set aside to deal with it include:

1. Has the teacher expressed positive or negative motives to deal with a particular pattern?

2. How fluent does the supervisor feel in his ability to explicate the pattern?

3. How fluently is the teacher likely to address it?

4. How logically or emotionally complex or simple does the pattern seem?

5. How sharply or distractedly is the teacher functioning at the moment?

6. How rewarding, innocuous, or threatening may the pattern prove?

7. How many data will be required to illustrate the pattern in question?

Common sense tells us that selectivity, being relative, can itself turn out to be too much if the few patterns selected are each too time-consuming to be handled together in one conference. Although supervisory issues tend to carry over from sequence to sequence of supervision, it often seems that some points are better than others for terminating a conference. It sometimes appears that even intermediate closure should occur at some special juncture of inquiry, not just any place. One problem, consequently, when considering the criterion of selectivity, is to project times and to make decisions accordingly.

Lest this seem altogether magical, we can think of parallel examples from teaching. It may be that the children are engaged in some social-studies unit that spans several weeks. The teacher is nonetheless likely to consider timing as he plans each day's activity—to plan his lessons so the students formulate some question by the end of Tuesday's work, discover some set of generalizations on Thursday, and define some relevant problems during Friday's session, for which they will prepare problem-solving strategies to present on Monday. Such planning need not be rigid or homogeneous, and might determine whether the pupils experience sufficient organization to maintain their focus. Similarly, good planning of conference time can spell the difference in benefits to the teacher.

The Principle of Energy Logical complexity, emotional loading, clarity of data, and the like will influence the amount of mental energy required to pursue specific issues in supervision. Recognizing this variable, the supervisor should avoid the likelihood that either member will become prematurely fatigued, by remembering selectivity. Once again, past experiences supervising the teacher represent the best index for judging outcomes of this kind.

The Principle of Sequence Whether or not the purposes of fewness are achieved may depend on the order in which selected patterns are broached in the conference. If, for example, patterns are ordered so that clear, logical transitions can be made from one context to the next, then, because such a conference should prove less exhausting and take less time than if such transitions were nonexistent, the goals of selectivity may be more readily achieved by following one sequence than another.

Supervisory transitions or the organizing principles behind sequences need not necessarily be substantive. They might, for example, be qualitative, progressing from weak patterns to strong ones. In any event, it is usually helpful to tell the teacher at the outset whether the sequence of issues to be broached in the conference is random or arranged in some fashion, to free him or her from the necessity of having to guess.

A simple statement such as, "There are a few things I thought we might get into, and it doesn't make any difference in what order we examine them," can save the teacher energy that might otherwise have been spent trying to guess the direction in which the conference was moving.

SUMMARY

■ In this chapter, our principal question has been how the supervisor reduces his or her complete analysis of the observational data by selecting specific patterns to treat in the conference. Our discussion has proceeded as though the supervisor's strategy was being dictated primarily by the press of data, rather than by general goals. Given an analyzed body of behavioral data, we suggest, selections should be based upon criteria of saliency, psychological accessibility, and selectivity (fewness). We have offered some rationales for this model, and some indication of what kinds of things supervisors might think about when attempting to make such decisions. Finally, we have emphasized that room must always be left open for new or different interpretations of data, until there remains no question about the validity and usefulness of a conclusion or discussion.

REFERENCES

[1] Thomas J. Sergiovanni and Robert J. Starratt, *Supervision: Human Perspectives*, 4th ed., McGraw-Hill, New York, 1988, pp. 225–237.

CHAPTER

8

The Supervisory Conference

In This Chapter

- Facilitating Success
- Interval Behavior
- Conference Conditions
- Opening
- Transition/Body
- Closing
- Summary

All the thought and energy the supervisor has invested in the pre-observation conference, observation, and analysis and strategy come to fruition in the supervisory conference.

The purposes of the supervisory conference include:

1. Defining and confirming teaching issues via lesson feedback.
2. Providing didactic help to improve future teaching. *And,*
3. Providing training in techniques of teacher self-improvement.

Strategic planning for the conference has been described in Chapter 7. This chapter is intended to be a hands-on, practical, generic guide to implement that strategic planning. It includes first, the conference's purposes and the supervisor's responsibility in fulfilling them. Several guidelines are presented for expectancies of supervisor behavior toward and interaction with the teacher in the interval between the observation and the supervisory conference. Next, a discussion between teachers reveals important conference-time and logistical considerations; added are supervisor behavior factors. Finally, the three conference components—the opening, the transition/body, and the closing—are concisely presented, with practical examples and suggestions given where appropriate.

FACILITATING SUCCESS

Facilitating Condition 10

The conference is a professional conversation, a privileged moment, to stretch for deeper understanding and enhanced skills that will in time help children to thrive in the school environment. The central purpose of the conference is to stimulate teacher instructional improvement by providing constructive lesson feedback to the teacher. The conference itself is an observable example of supervisory behavior, especially by the teacher who may decide whether or not the supervisor is interested in and can facilitate supervision necessary for his or her instructional improvement. Consider this example.

The setting is the fifth-grade pod of an elementary school, separated from the other pods and from the main building by connecting outside covered walkways. There are four fifth-grade teachers. Two of them team-teach in social sciences and open the folding wall between their respective classrooms to form a large group instruction room. They have complemented each other well during the past six years.

The supervisor observed and videotaped their team-taught lesson, and effected a FIAC analysis of it. Having completed analysis and strategy, the supervisor planned to be somewhat indirect in the conference. When the teachers arrived, they seemed nervous and the supervisor tried to be as supportive as possible in setting the stage for a positive conference. As the teachers viewed the tape, the supervisor pointed out positive aspects of the lesson to them and praised them for their interaction skills, but the teachers seemed unwilling to react to the supervisor's comments. After the tape, the supervisor asked the teachers' opinions, and they responded with such comments as "This was an excellent lesson," and "We are well pleased with it."

Sensing that all was not well, the supervisor departed from the planned strategy, asked if the teachers wished to view again any part of the lesson, and then attempted to highlight and praise several more positive aspects of the teaching. But their response was minimal. Rather than going into an analysis of each teacher's part in the lesson from the FIAC matrices, the supervisor suggested that they end the conference for that afternoon and perhaps look at certain aspects of the taped lesson again tomorrow. At first the teachers were reluctant, but finally they agreed to this suggestion.

The supervisor met with the teachers again the next day. One of the teachers opened by stating, "You know, we had little, if any, sleep last night. We previously heard that you were observing at our school to determine which two teachers you would fire. We didn't want to be the two and that's why we didn't react very much yesterday. But as we talked with each other and with our spouses last night, we finally realized that what we were told could not have been true, judging from the facilitative way you worked with us yesterday. We are now ready to work with you on the analysis of our lesson." This example illustrates, among other things, the need for the supervisor to be flexible, both procedurally and emotionally.

The central purpose of the conference is to provide constructive objective feedback to the teacher for improvement of future teaching. Conference goals are predetermined, for the most part, by the stages of CS leading up to the conference and by the supervisor-teacher relationship. The supervisor retains the primary responsibility to:

- Ensure that the goals are reached.
- Maintain the pace of the conference.
- Cope with problems that arise. *And,*
- Decide when to either (a) depart from the planned strategy, if that strategy fails, or (b) terminate the conference.

The supervisor should consider these responsibilities integral to the CS process. In the example above, the supervisor clearly accepted these responsibilities. Instead of pursuing in the initial conference what was rapidly becoming a struggle, the supervisor suggested the conference be continued the next day. This approach succeeded since, during the intervening time, the supervisor reflected and planned further, and the teachers themselves were persuaded that the supervisor's motives and manner of working with them discounted their earlier fears.

Role training for conferencing is helpful for supervisors. In learning about roles, we believe it is better to be aware of the many options available and to learn how and under what circumstances it is best to use them. Building rapport, establishing trust, and learning how to offer certain kinds of questions, interpretations, and reflections of the teacher's feelings are essential. Automaton-like technical behavior should be avoided at all costs. If CS is to succeed, both teacher and supervisor must understand and accept their and each other's respective roles, and both must understand their interactive roles. Both parties can learn to accept, appreciate, and understand the implications and responsibilities of each other's roles. Once roles are established, the supervisor may help train the teacher to self-supervise by experimenting with some role interchange in the conference. With practice, roles may be better effected by both parties. A teacher's defense mechanisms may become less pronounced through this process; a supervisor's understanding of the "hows" and "whys" of those defense mechanisms may deepen, improving the supervisor's ability to successfully cope with them.

INTERVAL BEHAVIOR

■ Events occurring in the interval between the observation and the conference can become, accidentally or by design, a help or a hindrance to the CS process. Some supervisors, aware of this possibility, seek to avoid any contact with teachers in that interval, while others deliberately take certain actions in the interval (remarks, gestures, dropping off notes, and so forth) as part of their communication strategy.

What is the optimum length of this interval? As a rule, the conference ought to be held as soon as possible after the observation; but sometimes a longer time may be needed for the supervisor to digest the data or for the teacher to be psychologically ready for the discussion. Regarding this interval, the supervisor should:

1. Include in the pre-observation conference agreement some arrangement about how to deal with interval contacts.
2. Take care when leaving an observation not to unintentionally communicate approval or disapproval.
3. Follow the agreed arrangement regarding interval contacts. *And,*
4. Never lose sight of the importance of rapport, and recognize that interval behavior is by its nature potentially hazardous to, or nurturing of, rapport maintenance.

CONFERENCE CONDITIONS

■ A group of experienced teachers in a graduate supervision class is discussing conference technology, and the question is raised: "What things should *always* be true about a supervisory conference?" Their responses may be of interest to you.

JANE : I want for it to be in a comfortable place—comfortable chairs, good lighting, bearable temperature, even some niceties such as pleasant drapes and a rug.

GEORGE: Well, yes, but even more important for me is the location. It should be convenient for me to get there . . . not too far from my classroom.

JACKSON: The supervisor's office?

GEORGE : Only if it's nearby.

JANE: Not me. I'd rather it *would* be in her office. She has a nice, quiet, comfortable, private place.

JACKSON: Yes, privacy is important. In your classroom you never know who will interrupt you.

MELVA: I think it's important that the conference should be a real sharing experience, not just a one-way message from on high.

JACKSON: Amen. And let's add: It should be free of evaluation. Maybe sometimes it can include evaluation, but I see the supervisory conference, especially in the ob cycle, as a *helping* activity.

JANE: Characterized by mutual respect.

JACKSON: Yes. And based on needs that I have, not so much the supervisor's.

MELVA: Our supervisor tries to arrange the chairs so that no one is in a dominant physical relationship to the other person.

JANE: How's that done?

MELVA: Well, she places two similar chairs next to each other, with a small coffee table between.

EVA: I'd worry more about the available time. He can sit on a throne as far as I'm concerned, but I hate it when he rushes me through the discussion.

GEORGE: Yeah. Time's important. Time pressure can really prevent the conference from reaching its goals, a comfortable closure.

JUAN: I'd also argue that the conference shouldn't happen just by itself.

JANE: What does that mean?

JUAN: Well, it shouldn't be the only one. There should be a regular history, and this one is just Chapter Six, let's say, in a ten-chapter book.

JACKSON: Book-of-the-Month?

JUAN: Well, yes, in a way. Book-of-the-Year, maybe. What I meant is that it's a continuous—or ongoing—kind of thing. I don't want just *one* conference to be all that important.

These teachers saw as important certain physical considerations (comfort, privacy, a good location, encouraging seating arrangements), adequate time, a helping and sharing relationship, the absence of evaluation pressure, and mutual acceptance and respect. Juan hit on another crucial idea, that each conference be part of a sequence. Thus, for optimal conference conditions, consider these factors:

Time The interval between observation and conference, the time of day to hold the conference, and the length of time to allow for the conference are all important considerations.

Logistics A pleasing and aesthetic surrounding for the conference, minimal distractions, seating arrangements, and resources all encourage rapport.

Content In data presentation, *how much*, *how*, and *when* are key considerations. For data analysis, ask: "What does it mean?" In data interpretation, ask: "Why is it occurring?" In developing alternatives, ask: "How many are available, and which one is best?" Finally, in goal selection, critical elements are how to select, who selects, and when and how to proceed.

Supervisor Behavior The supervisor's verbal and non-verbal behavior plays an important role. Ideally, the supervisor should, over time, develop a varied and extensive repertory of words, phrases, and tactics to communicate intended messages. Verbal communication, especially in conferences, is crucial. Some interaction analysis systems measure teacher talk. Some, as the FIAC we describe in Chapter 6, break the talk into categories such as direct (lecturing to, telling someone to do something, or criticizing) and indirect (asking, praising, encouraging, and accepting feelings). And although FIAC is not intended to measure non-verbal communication, a nod of the head, pat on the shoulder, or smile can be recorded as encouraging. Perhaps we might use an instrument or combination of instruments to analyze interaction in conferences. Videotape would be excellent, perhaps complemented by FIAC (for categorizing purposes, the supervisor replaces the teacher, and the teacher replaces the student). As supervisors, we encourage teachers to ask more questions of students, praise and encourage them, and develop their self-esteem; likewise, supervisors must do the same with teachers. When we confer, we should encourage ideas from the teachers and not monopolize the conference. O, the beauty of videotape!

Some experts claim that non-verbal communication can comprise up to 80 percent of your message in a one-to-one conversation. Body language can convey moods, attitudes, approval, deception, and status. And non-verbal discounting (that is, behavior which is incongruent with accompanying verbal behavior) can quickly destroy rapport and supervisory effectiveness.

The face, hands, head, limbs, and trunk all convey messages in decreasing importance. Facial cues are the single most important source of non-verbal communication. The eyes ("the windows of the soul," in the words of John Greenleaf Whittier) tell a lot. We suggest that in a one-on-one conference with a teacher you make as much eye contact as possible. Tactile non-verbal communication also tells a lot. And how we as supervisors interpret and send messages about personal and social distance, territory or bubble of space, apparel (clothing, jewelry, cosmetics), and posture makes a difference in our effectiveness. We encourage the reader to seek out the excellent works of such authors as Harold Barnard, Paul Byers, Charles Galloway, Ira Gordon, Edward T. Hall, Dorothy Hennings, Carl Rogers, and Aaron Wolfgang for more detailed information on non-verbal communication.

Some of these conference variables will have been decided upon in the pre-observation session and may even have been included in the agreement, such as when and where to meet. The choice may have been made by teacher, supervisor, or both. If not, the supervisor may have made such decisions during the analysis and strategy session.

OPENING

■ There are at least three events in each conference:

The Opening

Words and actions intentionally used by the supervisor in the initial minutes of the conference.

The Transition/Body

Words and actions that signal the supervisor is ready to (and does) describe and discuss pre-conference objectives, lesson observations, analysis, and plans for future improvement. *And,*

The Closing

The concluding action that links the conference outcome with the post-conference analysis.

The opening should be based on a plan that includes anticipating how the teacher will react to a given action and having a stand-by plan ready to cope with each possible teacher reaction. Consider these examples:

Action Ask the teacher what he or she thought about the lesson.
Consequence Be prepared for such responses ranging from "Oh, I thought it was terrible—did you, too?" to "I feel just great—this was one of the best lessons I taught, right?" to "Hey, wait a minute—it's *your* job to tell me what *you* think!"

Action Ask for additional data. "What happened in the class after I left? I'm curious. Did Jimmy actually finish his project? How did the kids do on the test?"
Consequence This data is useful if the supervisor needs extra information to support an emerging hypothesis or recommendation. It may also reduce some of the teacher's tensions or at least create a moment when he or she can volunteer information beyond what was requested.

Action Recapitulate the pre-observation agreement. Then deal with data pertaining to these items one by one in the order in which they were listed.

Consequence Be prepared for any type of response. You may get very positive feedback or defensive reactions.

Action Plunge directly into the data, presenting whatever objective data are available.
Consequence Let some of the conclusions or implications flow from them. The supervisor may in such an instance wait for teacher questions or interpretations, or both, to emerge before discussing his or her own assessments.

Action Play part or all of a videotape or audiotape.
Consequence This enables the teacher to review certain events that, during analysis, the supervisor considered important to the agreed-on instructional improvement goal. One version of this approach, which in some schools is standard procedure, is to have the teacher review the tape in the interval between observation and conference, to prepare some self-analysis for the conference.

Action Start off on a positive note.
Consequence If the data are basically positive, determining an opening tactic is less difficult. However, positive overkill is also possible. End with the most sobering news.

Action Start with the not-so-good news, then switch to the more positive data.
Consequence See what happens.

Action Try the *laissez-faire* ("let them do as they choose") approach.
Consequence This is not an acceptable tactic very often. However, there are some defensible ways for the supervisor to effect a *laissez-faire* approach. Have a series of conferences, rather than just one, following an observation, holding part of the conference on one day and the remaining parts on others. Each conference can focus on only a few items of the lesson so as not to overwhelm the teacher.

The opening depends to a great degree on the supervisor's working relationship with the teacher. Determining openings is likely to be more important in the early working stages of the supervisor-teacher relationship than after the supervisor has worked with the teacher over a period of time. After the supervisor has established trust and conducted many conferences, he or she generally develops a sense of how the teacher is likely to deal with tension-inducing questions and react to supervisory strategies. Yet the supervisor must always be conscious of, and thoroughly plan for, the conference opening, irrespective of the trust and rapport relationship with the teachers.

TRANSITION/BODY

- The supervisor seeks in the conference to:
  - Respond to the teacher's perceived morale and state of mind.
  - Offer appropriate reinforcement.
  - Provide data relating to the questions and concerns of the teacher.
  - Keep the conference discussion within boundaries that make sense at that moment for that teacher. *And,*
  - Most importantly, nurture and encourage the teacher's capacity for professional self-growth, through a growth plan with specific roles and responsibilities for both supervisor and teacher.

The transition/body of the conference is the "make-or-break" stage. Supervisors must work very hard to see that the teacher believes and trusts in their attempt to comprehend the teacher's professional experiences in his or her own terms. The supervisor's goal should be that teachers are not left with feelings such as these:

> "It's just a lot of talk. We never seem to get anything done and sometimes I can't see what we're after."
>
> "I'd be much better off having that time for planning and for reading pupils' papers."
>
> "I never feel there's time to fully understand what the supervisor's trying to show me. And so I often don't have anything to say, and then I feel kind of stupid."
>
> "We seem to spend a great deal of time just talking about what we're doing, you know? That is, besides just doing things, the supervisor keeps talking about doing things: why we should do them, and how we're doing them, and things like that."
>
> "Sometimes I get the feeling that the supervisor really feels that [the teaching] stinks, but that he has to find something good to

> say about it anyhow. I'd feel a lot better if the supervisor would just come right out and say when things are good or bad."

But if conferences generate frustrations of this kind, various concerns about trust and understanding are inevitable. Failing to recognize these concerns constitutes a hazard in conferencing.

Given a successful opening, the transition to the body of the conference is crucial. Transitions are situational and no two are alike. Short or long, they determine the success of the conference body, the time when pre-conference objectives, lesson observation, and analysis are discussed with a view to planning for future improvement. That planning must be precise, containing specific goals to be reached and methods to attain them.

Conference body concerns are generally difficult to illustrate by short excerpts, but are nevertheless vivid and common. For example: Faulty techniques, weak conceptualizations of the CS model, or emotional or intellectual deficits that interfere with the supervisor's performance will tend to leave the teacher with a negative feeling about supervision.

The supervisor must perform many functions simultaneously:

- Listen to what the teacher is saying, and understand his or her meanings—both intended and underlying.
- Listen to his or her own inner voices, motives, impulses, values, and professional biases as they rise up to influence his or her mental responses and behavior.
- Maintain an awareness of prior strategies, and engage in behavior consistent with the intended outcomes.
- Transform ideas and intentions into actions.
- Draw upon technical expertise.
- Function by the specialized conventions of the CS discipline.
- Deal with substantive curricular issues.
- Be self-reflective and insightful, and devote as much energy to self-examination as to examination and analysis of the teacher's work.
- Perform counseling and didactic functions, and know which compromises between diagnostic and "treatment" goals are best at any given juncture in the supervision. *And,*
- Be committed to process goals as well as to substantive technical outcomes.

The list above is by no means complete. We supplement it with a list of suggested *Do's* and *Don'ts* for further emphasis.

DO	DON'T
Take an active lead in analyzing teaching and developing strategies for its modification.	Make teachers overly dependent on you.
Use the most productive process.	Misjudge process or timing.
Use data effectively.	Be redundant or examine excessively.
Be accepting and supportive.	Confuse intentions with effects.
Identify cause and effect properly.	Create intellectual closure and inquiry.
Make suggestions.	Make too many suggestions.
Be cautious with value judgments.	Use unexamined value judgments.
Be objective.	Lose sight of your strategies through self-anxiety.
Look for causes, not symptoms of teacher defensiveness.	Be psychologically defensive or threatened.
Be sensitive.	Judge prematurely.
Be flexible but focused.	Be inconsistent or unprepared.
Recognize your capabilities.	Try to be indispensable.

CLOSING

■ The closing is the concluding action linking conference outcomes with the post-conference analysis. In the transition/body of the conference, the supervisor and teacher review the lesson and its objective data, and discuss an improvement plan. The closing then is a link to, and functions in a way similar in content and process to, the pre-observation conference. The closing should review the process of "this is what happened" with "this is what we want to happen," and provide an agreement stating,

"This is how we will make it happen." It sets objectives and process for the next supervision cycle and determines both the supervisor's and teacher's roles in the improvement process.

The supervisor has presented data from the observed lesson and compared espoused objectives from the pre-observation conference to actual performance. The teacher has reviewed the data with the supervisor and helped create the improvement plan. The closing presents an opportunity to firm up or confirm the plan, assess ownership of the plan, and provide direction to the plan. Therefore the closing reflects the success of the opening and transition/body phases of the supervisory conference. To close the conference successfully, the supervisor must:

- Be sensitive and flexible enough to move in the teacher's direction.
- Be an exemplar of strategies espoused for the teacher. *And,*
- Be directed to both immediate and long-range goals.

SUMMARY

■ All the thought and energy invested by the supervisor in the pre-observation conference, observation, and analysis and strategy comes to fruition in the supervisory conference. The conference defines and confirms (through supervisory and objective data) feedback on lesson foci, provides didactic help for improving future teaching, and provides training in techniques of teacher self-improvement.

Planning conference conditions (such as time, logistics, content, and supervisor behavior) are essential to success. Separating the conference into three events—the opening, the transition/body, and the closing—provides both supervisor and teacher with a framework from which data can be reviewed and improvement planned. Role delineation is crucial throughout the process, and teacher self-supervision is an ideal goal for both supervisor and teacher. For successful conferences we, as supervisors, must be well-trained in both the ideas and methods of CS work; moreover, we must have a great capacity for interacting, learning, and changing.

CHAPTER

9

THE POST-CONFERENCE ANALYSIS

In This Chapter

- Facilitating Success
- Guidelines
- Implementing
- Summary

Evaluating the clinical supervision cycle stages, from pre-observation conference to supervisory conference, is essential, because how well the process operates in the future is determined, in large measure, by the success of the present CS cycle. This chapter is the last of five describing the individual stages of the cycle. It is intended to be a hands-on, practical guide to planning and implementing the post-conference analysis. It includes, first, a rationale for supervisor self-improvement through post-conference analysis. Next, guidelines are presented, as are implementing strategies, with questions and discussions for strategies. Finally, a general summary of the five-stage cycle is presented.

FACILITATING SUCCESS

■ Perhaps the best way to improve a practitioner's informal and formal professional work is to receive feedback periodically from peers and constituents. This is especially true in CS, for it is all but impossible to imagine a rational double-standard that could free supervisors from the necessity of being supervised themselves. Teachers should retain the love of learning and engage in self-improvement activities. By retaining the role of learner, they become even better teachers. Supervisors in turn should retain the roles of teacher and learner. The post-conference analysis focuses on improvement of the *supervisor's* performance. By accepting that, supervisors improve both their supervisory concepts and techniques, and keep in focus the teacher's perspective of the supervision process, thus becoming even better supervisors.

Supervisory critiques originally arose in training situations where group supervision was being practiced and where, consequently, it was easy for each supervisor to be observed and analyzed by his or her peers. Under such conditions, the model of supervision we have been examining in relation to instruction could be applied, with little alteration, to supervision. In most scholastic settings today, supervision is not conducted in groups, although the continued expansion of team-teaching, on both the elementary and secondary school levels, creates possibilities for multiple supervision that should be welcomed and facilitated by modern school administrators. We invite the reader to review the section in Chapter 3 on teaming, and particularly the section in Chapter 4 on peer supervision, which provides recommendations for practice.

For the present, however, we will generally deal with situations in which supervision is conducted by one supervisor with one teacher at a time. Although we can imagine various arrangements in which teachers (and even pupils) participate in supervising the supervisor (we think that supervision's future urgently requires these innovations), our immediate and practical question might be simply how supervisors can supervise themselves on a regular and systematic basis.

For best self-supervision results, we suggest videotaping supervision conferences for analysis, and collecting notes and thoughts of the entire CS process effected. Subsequent to the post-conference analysis, the supervisor can use other objective instrumentation to gather valuable data from the videotape. The supervisor should seek all possible sources of objective data gathering from the post-conference analysis to provide information for his or her growth and improvement as a supervisor. Once these data have been collected, the supervisor uses the information in essentially the same way as he or she uses classroom data. The post-conference analysis can represent a highly abridged process, involving only an analysis of the supervision that has taken place and the subsequent planning based upon such analysis. We recommend the frequent use of a post-conference analysis session conducted with the teacher or others present as active participants in the process.

GUIDELINES

Facilitating Condition 11

The post-conference analysis is a new and different event. It is primarily a supervisor self-improvement mechanism whose purposes include:

1. Assessment of the supervisory conference, in terms of (a) the teacher's criteria, as determined in the pre-observation conference, (b) the supervisory criteria, and (c) the apparent value of the conference to the teacher.

2. Evaluation of the supervisor's skill in handling the various phases of the cycle.

In a sense, this post-conference analysis represents supervision's "superego"—its conscience. It provides a basis for assessing whether the supervisor and CS are working. Ideally, the post-conference analysis should comprise both of the following:

A Tête-à-Tête Session Between Supervisor and Teacher In the tête-à-tête session the supervisor and teacher jointly examine the pluses and minuses of supervision techniques used, the implicit and explicit assumptions made, the values and emotional variables considered, and the technical and process goals effected. Data obtained from this examination assist the supervisor in making decisions to modify his or her practices to better meet both the teacher's and supervisor's future needs. Participation in this part of the observation cycle enhances the supervisor's efforts to understand the intellectual and emotional dimensions of the teacher's work.

The Supervisor's Private Self-Reflective Session The self-reflective session is a private activity that takes place after the tête-à-tête discussion. It involves a full, objective review of everything the supervisor did or failed to do during the clinical cycle, through questions such as these:

- How skillfully did I conduct the pre-observation conference?
- Was the teacher sufficiently at ease and forthcoming, so that real and important problems surfaced for examination?
- Was a good plan developed for the observation, and were both parties comfortable with the agreement?
- Was my behavior during the observation consistent with the teacher's expectations?
- Was I sufficiently skillful in perceiving and making an objective record of what happened during observation?
- While I was observing, did I succeed in understanding what happened and its significance?
- Did my analysis, and the strategy I worked out for conducting the post-observation conference, make reasonable sense?
- Did the conference succeed as a professionally useful experience for the teacher?
- Did we end up with a greater understanding of the teacher's professional strengths, as well as valid perceptions of how those strengths can be increased?
- Is the teacher-supervisor relationship at least as positive and as forward-looking as it was before the cycle?

- What did I learn about my own supervisory talents and tendencies, and what changes should I make to do a better job?
- How well do I understand the repetitive patterns of my own supervisory behavior?
- What effort should I make to change those patterns?

These are some of the questions the supervisor might address while wrapping up the cycle just completed and preparing to participate in future ones.

Perhaps the principal problem of self-supervision is objectivity: the problem of looking at our work from a proper distance, and performing an analysis likely to be worth something. As participant and observer, the clinical supervisor's role in the post-conference analysis is difficult indeed, since the observer (supervisor) is of necessity both detached and effectively participating and sharing in face-to-face relationships with a teacher, peer, or others in the process. Self-supervision is thus doubly difficult; while we must strive to be objective, we are also turning our attention toward our own behavior and looking at our output in very fine detail. What could be more difficult than to maintain distance in an activity that requires intense concentration upon one's own behavior?

IMPLEMENTING

■ If both the supervision conference and tête-à-tête session are taped, post-conference analysis becomes potentially more powerful for improving future cycles. We suggest the following procedures for viewing and analyzing those tapes:

1. Try to establish a lack of self-consciousness by casually watching enough videotape to become accustomed to yourself, your voice, and your mannerisms, so that you can view it with a degree of objectivity.
2. Try to be particularly aware of episodes in the supervision about which you feel very positive or very negative. Assume that strong evaluative feelings tend to be global and incorporate "halo effects," so that you can try to pay particular attention to those episodes about which your feelings seem least equivocal.
3. As you examine the tape for the second or third time, pay special attention to the teacher's words and inflections, and try very hard to discipline yourself against projecting your feelings upon the teacher. Try to break free of your own feelings and listen to the

teacher's responses, to see what clues they provide about how he or she was responding to your behavior, or feeling about things generally.

4. Seek opinions for collaborative analysis of critical episodes; ask others to listen "cold" and to tell you what they hear.

5. It may even be beneficial to go *directly* to the source if you feel that it is important enough to matter (and if it does not interfere with what you are after in the supervision) and replay problematic episodes *for the teacher*, to better learn the significance they may carry for him or her. Although no such method is foolproof, it is sometimes very useful to take such pains, especially when they protect you from proceeding on false assumptions concerning the teacher's experiences in supervision.

6. Besides listening with special acuity to "hot" and "cold" spots, try to stay alert to long passages of tape that feel flat and featureless. More often than not, flatness is in the ear or eye of the listener, and what is actually flat is the supervisor's perceptual apparatus or level of intellectual energy for finding the meaning of the teacher's behavior (flattened by the supervisor's own anxiety or defensive blocking). Try to overcome this by forcing attention on "grey" episodes. When you find your mind wandering, try to set it straight again by listening and re-listening to the episode it has wandered from, until you feel relatively certain that you have heard whatever there is to hear and found whatever you are likely to find there.

Just as our analyses of teaching behavior generally require us to search for likely incidental learnings by trying to assume the pupils' frames of reference as they experienced the lesson, in the post-conference analysis we should try to use the same techniques for calculating our effects upon the teacher. A constant question should be, "What might the teacher have been learning at any given moment in the conference as a result of my supervisory behavior?" Again, the unrelenting problem is to keep as distinct as possible the contrast between what the supervisor would have learned had he or she been the teacher and what, indeed, the teacher might have actually experienced.

Questions in Implementing

We should try to stay especially alert to certain questions, such as the following, that have proven critical in many post-conference analyses:

Question Where does the locus of initiative for supervisory inquiry tend to be?

Discussion When either the teacher or the supervisor consistently initiates supervisory issues and the other does not, the imbalance of initiative may signify unproductive processes that tend to reinforce resistance to inquiry or excessive dependency upon the supervisor for structure and direction.

Question What kinds of rewards tend to be provided?
Discussion Supervisory behavior may need to be modified appropriately if it appears, for example, that:

- Intended rewards are not experienced as such by the teacher.
- Rewards tend to be more social than substantive.
- An implicit expectation of negativeness (or some sort of implied punishment) has become established as a motivational element in the teacher's work.
- Initially potent rewards have become ineffectual through excessive use. *And,*
- Except in the supervisory interaction, the teacher experiences a paucity of rewards in his or her professional work, and is at a loss to envision activities from which they will be generated.

Question What is the proportion of questions in each participant's dialogue (and what are the questions' formal characteristics)?
Discussion A preponderance of questions may reflect avoidance of problem-solving activity. Excessive questioning by the supervisor may create a feeling of interrogation; excessive questioning by the teacher may reflect excessive dependence upon the supervisor for answers. The formal structure of questions may be identified as a source of frustration, inefficiency, or, on the other hand, of positive achievements in supervision.

Question Whose deeds are most abundant in the conference?
Discussion For example, who drafts whatever plans are laid for future teaching? If the supervisor is the sole devisor of plans, strategies, or techniques that the teacher subsequently employs, the supervisor may begin to confuse enthusiasm for his or her own notions with objective appraisal of the teacher's performance.

Question Does the behavior of either participant become stereotyped?

Discussion In addition to reward patterns, other elements of supervision may become stereotyped. When supervisory procedures become purely ritualistic, their utility is bound to decline. We have generally found it useful in post-conference analysis to examine whether any activity, whether in the teaching or the conference, has taken place solely "as a matter of course."

Question How abundant are explicit rationales for value judgments and for decisions affecting future work?
Discussion The teacher's or supervisor's proceeding, regularly, on the basis of unexamined value judgments and decisions, would oppose the rational analysis for clinical supervision. The supervisor should never suggest that the value (or lack thereof) of specific techniques rests on the sheer fact that either the supervisor or teacher likes or dislikes them.

Question How likely is it that semantic confusion (or the general ambiguity of language) has created illusions of agreement or disagreement?
Discussion Such uncertainties have frequently led to the more extensive use of playbacks in future supervision conferences.

When we have done the job fully and have prepared our supervision (of the teacher) by planning explicit substantive and process goals and cognitive outcomes, then we should be in the best possible position to undertake a productive post-conference analysis. Goals generate a structure within which it is relatively efficient to evaluate what took place; they represent a set of more or less delimiting categories in which to focus examination.

It is, of course, possible to perform a post-conference analysis without having videotaped the supervision. Doing so, however, is more difficult, less efficient, and less trustworthy. The more memory work required, the more distortion occurs, and the less valid are the processes and outcomes of our self-analysis. The more actual data available, the better our chances are of achieving something useful from our efforts. Besides, planning for the next sequence of supervision often is confirmed in the post-conference analysis.

Question How frequently should we conduct post-conference analysis? Should we do it with every observation cycle?
Discussion In actual practice, not even the most committed supervisors are likely to have enough time or psychic endurance to postanalyze every sequence of supervision in which they function. Nor, one suspects, would it be necessary or useful for us to do such extensive analysis any more than it would be desirable to apply our complete model of clinical

supervision in every instance of supervision. As in most other human and professional endeavors, the question becomes one of determining how often and how much and at what moments a potentially useful activity should be undertaken. We have not found any certain answers, but we do think there are guidelines that can be followed:

- Perform the post-conference analysis at some arbitrary interval (e.g., in conjunction with every fourth or fifth sequence of supervision).
- Employ a conference analysis at the conclusion of a supervisory cycle or, depending on the difficulty and complexity of the supervision in question.
- Employ a conference analysis during the initial sequences in a cycle.

Whatever the decision, the post-conference analysis is most likely to succeed when it involves the participation of a second supervisor, if only because under such conditions the supervisor is relieved of some of the burden of keeping himself or herself realistically objective.

Question What should the teacher's role be in this analysis?
Discussion Unless there are important contraindications, we are especially enthusiastic about having the observed teacher fill the role of "supervisor's supervisor" at propitious moments, because:

- No one is more likely to have pertinent information about the supervisor's effects than the teacher so affected.
- It provides desirable role reversals on a regular and dependable basis.
- It relieves some status anxieties of supervision.
- It cuts across real and imaginary hierarchies.
- It enhances the teacher's feeling of dignity in the supervisory relationship.
- It enables the teacher to gain higher degrees of objective distance on his or her own work. *And,*
- It keeps the supervisor fully aware of the effects of supervisory techniques and strategies.

The teacher stands to gain some supervisory competency and consequently stands to become a more potent and valuable member of the school faculty.

Problems in Implementing

Although there is no clear-cut methodology for self-supervision, the post-conference analysis should not be considered simply a collection of good intentions and ritualistic motions. *The post-conference analysis should afford a time for professional self-examination that exists for the profession's good, for the supervisor's own growth and development, and for the teacher's protection and advantage.*

It is probably true that all persons must work out the incentives and tools of self-examination for themselves, and that no one can chart the engagement that should occur for all persons as they search to improve. Even the ideal supervisor cannot ensure self-analysis success. We can think of no better way to express this understanding than by expressing the types of things that can go wrong.

Problem The supervisor feels, in a sweeping fashion, that he or she does—or does not—know what he or she is doing, and thus in either case shrugs his or her shoulders, and avoids examining self-behavior closely as a way of understanding more clearly what the trouble is.
Discussion There are various ways to express the basic difficulties of this stage. There is always the problem of engaging an objective distance with one's own work and one's own behavior. In this connection, many specific problems may be pinned to the various defenses that operate in human personalities to obscure, to deny, to rationalize, to avoid reality, often in the same manner for all of us but always differing in detail from one individual to another.

In our own experience and in those of colleagues with whom we have been closely associated, we often find that supervisors feel consciously afraid to look inward. When "being scared" does not exist explicitly, the underlying anxiety is variously experienced, either as fatigue ("I really believe in the post-conference analysis but, generally, by the time I've finished going through a whole sequence of supervision, I'm just too pooped to get involved in one") or as an absence of motivation ("There really didn't seem to be any need for self-analysis; I mean, it wasn't as if it had been a particularly complex sequence up until then").

Problem The neophyte supervisor may feel he or she has inadequate analytical skills.

Discussion When supervisors are not competent to interpret behavioral data generally, there is no reason to expect them to be particularly competent in analyzing their own behavior. From time to time, incidentally, we have observed an interesting related phenomenon: that some supervisors were, in fact, highly capable of performing insightful analyses of their own work but were less capable of analyzing teachers' work and of conducting conferences based upon such analyses. In such cases it has usually appeared that supervisors' problems, even in Stage 3 (analysis and strategy), derived from anxieties around confrontation. This says that besides lacking the fortitude for confrontations in the conference, supervisors could not even adequately design strategies for themselves for prospective confrontations during the strategy stage.

Problem In yet another sense, failure to achieve successful post-conference analysis frequently seems associated with a simple lack of self-discipline that is expressed in other manifestations of sloppiness throughout the supervisor's work.
Discussion The very same supervisor whose observation notes are slipshod is likely to be the person who forgets or declines to employ a tape recorder during the conference. Inadequate self-discipline is, however, more likely to be expressed by the habit of promising oneself that although there really is insufficient time or energy to perform a post-conference analysis today, one will definitely do so tomorrow—or the next day, or the next. Lazily, some supervisors also do not bother to specify behavioral outcomes and behavioral criteria for successful conferences beforehand and, consequently, reduce the certainty and efficiency with which they might otherwise evaluate conferences retroactively.

Problem Sometimes supervisors repress data about their own performance. Sometimes, although the data are admitted to consciousness, they are processed through defensive filters. Sometimes supervisors' findings are influenced by temperamental factors, for example, when a self-deprecatory analysis emanates from a spell of gloomy despondence.
Discussion Even when supervisors are able to perform an adequate evaluation of their work, unless they are blessed by the existence of colleagues whom they may employ as professional foils, they are often frustrated, if not hamstrung, by the difficulties involved in progressing from psychic realizations to behavioral modifications. As a rule, their opportunities for rehearsal are not nearly so abundant as those they may provide for their supervisees. While self-supervision represents a highly valued practice to us, ironically, perhaps, once such activity has been established on a systematic basis, it generally seems that the requirement for *other* people to participate in the process becomes more pressing. This is the principal

sense in which we believe that supervisors never become obsolete: The more autonomously the teacher engages in self-supervision, the more productively he or she can employ the supervisor's services, and the same holds true for supervision of supervision.

Although such phenomena have not appeared with great frequency in our work, certain other peculiarities arise from time to time in relation to post-conference analysis. Some supervisors employ the idea that ultimately post-conference analyses are performed for the supervisees' sake, and they manage, by that rationale, to escape genuinely productive involvement in a process also intended to be for their own benefit. One thinks, analogously, of parents, in child guidance clinics, who agree to enter psychotherapeutic treatment of their own, but who do so primarily because such treatment represents a condition set by the clinic for accepting their children. They say something like, "If we enter treatment grudgingly in order for our children or our spouse to be offered the treatment we believe them to need, then the therapeutic effects of our own treatment experience are likely not to materialize very substantially."

Problem Sometimes supervisors may spend too much of their energy in thinking about their own behavior and not enough in thinking about the teachers' needs and interests.

Discussion Self-analysis on the part of a supervisor is important, but the chief reason it is important is that it could lead to improvement in the ways teachers are served. We remain convinced that post-conference analyses are most likely to succeed in a context of group supervision or in a training program in which other supervisory personnel are available to participate, on a regular basis, in supervising the supervisor. For individual supervisors working alone, the problem of engaging in systematic self-examination will never be an easy one to resolve. Nonetheless, we cannot overstate the urgency of such activity if clinical supervision is truly to emerge as a potent and useful professional practice.

SUMMARY

■ No matter how CS is defined, it represents efforts on the part of both the supervisor and the supervisee to consider how professional performance can be well understood and then improved upon. In this volume we have constantly emphasized the helping, growth-inducing, analytical functions of supervision and have deliberately separated those functions from such administrative functions as judging, evaluating, and making personnel decisions. The latter are of course important, but it is in a human-resource-department context that CS activities are the most relevant.

Successful supervision is seen here as a continuing series of five-stage cycles, each providing background for the next, and all focusing on well-identified goals or objectives (both long-range and immediate). We regard as essential the establishment of good rapport between the parties involved, within which there is mutual understanding, mutual trust, and mutual ambitions for goal attainment. Fruitful observation requires that there also be mutual awareness (best cultivated through a well-versed pre-observation conference) of the teacher's intentions and expectations, and of the role the supervisor can best play in checking out their accomplishment.

There is almost no limit to the possibilities within the observation itself for the apperception, identification, recognition, and absorption of potentially useful information. Even the world's most skilled classroom observer will sometimes fail to see, hear, or even sense, something happening. On the other hand, the data-collection repertory of expert observers, no less than beginners, is always increasing. Yet creative invention of new techniques should not interfere with respecting the scope and the limits of the "contract" that governs the cycle. Nor is it allowable for the supervisor to be intrusive or distracting, except in those rare instances where such intrusion may have been planned. Even more sinful, in our view, is for the observer to permit opinions or judgments to surface in his or her mind before there has been adequate time for review of gathered data.

We hope the reader shares our enthusiasm for the third stage of the cycle, during which high-level intellectual analysis of observed events leads to high-level planning for the post-observation conference that lies ahead. One reason that we value observations by *teams* of observers is that the sharing of data and the collaborative examination of options and possibilities is both exhilarating and educating. However, even as a solo operation, the analysis and strategy session has a distinctly exciting and challenging dimension to it.

The professional conversation that ensues, which we describe as a privileged moment, can be like the satisfying final act of a play or the climax of an orchestral work. Did the performance take place as planned? In what ways did it succeed? In what ways could we have improved upon it? What have we learned about our "audience" and how better to serve its needs and expectations? Do some different scenarios now come to mind? What fine-tuning will make sense next time? What do we feel best about?

Next, with the curtain down and the actors or musicians musing in their dressing rooms about how things went, there is opportunity to put one's creative conscience to work. Some of the post-cycle analysis takes place in private, and some in mutual discussion. The overall purpose is to examine what happened and thereby to extend one's understanding of possibilities for the future.

CHAPTER

10

Clinical Supervision Today

In This Chapter

- Emphasis
- Use in Schools
- The Supervisor's Role
- Rapport and Mutual Trust
- Literature Emphasis
- Observation Methodology
- Summary: Toward the Future

This chapter looks at clinical supervision today. Presented first is a table describing recent progression of six aspects of CS: emphasis, use in schools, supervisor role, rapport and mutual trust, literature emphasis, and observation methodology.

TABLE 3

SIX ASPECTS OF CLINICAL SUPERVISION CONSIDERED BY DECADE

DECADE:	1970s	1980s	1990s
Emphasis:	Method	Concept and Method	Synthesize Method and Concept via Facilitating Conditions
Use in Schools:	Little	Little	Emergence
Supervisor Role:	Traditional	Improvement/ Management of Instruction	Collegial (Qualities of an Effective Supervisor)
Rapport and Mutual Trust:	Cursory	Supportive Role	Crucial
Literature Emphasis:	Little	Chapter in Supervision Texts	Increased
Observation Methodology:	Authoritarian	Interactive Means	Objective Analysis Systems

Next, we review the impact of each of these CS aspects on schools and instructional improvement. Finally, we take a look into the future.

EMPHASIS

■ We are strongly convinced, like Morris Cogan (in particular) and others, that many of the weaknesses in American schools today can be solved through universal application of effective supervision, through which teachers could be assisted toward better performance and a clearer vision of what improvements are possible. With such assistance, teachers could cope much more effectively with the difficult problems they face, and in turn we might well see a reversal of some of the statistics about the schools and their impact. We are persuaded that such efforts must include clinical supervisors who can work with teachers and curriculum so that students can be the recipients of an education of the highest quality possible.

The emphasis of CS today is to synthesize method and concept via facilitating conditions. In Chapter 3 we presented a conceptual background for CS and throughout this text we affirm that CS is both concept and method. Without an understanding of CS concept, the method cannot reach its full potential.

The eleven facilitating conditions, listed below and previously discussed in Chapters 4 through 9, emphasize the synthesis of CS concept and method:

1. Specific, achievement-oriented, school-wide improvement goals are in place.

2. The teacher has immediate as well as long-range objectives for strengthening his or her own classroom performance.

3. A growth plan (with a target objective, a timeline, and progress checks) has been established.

4. The supervisor or coach and teacher understand each other and the work context; interpersonal decoding is not necessary.

5. "The past is prologue"; previous episodes provide background.

6. Pre-observation agreement is respected as a contract.

7. The observer's presence is minimally distracting to students.

8. The observer's apperceptive skills and data-gathering tools are employed at full speed.

9. The observer postpones judgments or conclusions until an objective basis is established.

10. The post-observation conference is a professional conversation, a privileged moment to stretch for deeper understandings.

11. The post-conference analysis is a new and different event.

USE IN SCHOOLS

■ Robert Krajewski's opening paragraph to the preface of the Winter 1976 *Journal of Research and Development in Education* describes even today the status of CS in schools:

> Conceived at Harvard University more than fifteen years ago, "clinical supervision," as it is commonly called, still remains primarily a latent force for the improvement of instruction. Written about, discussed, taught and sometimes attempted, clinical supervision has yet to be fully born to the world of public education, K–12. Scholars and practitioners alike have made valiant efforts to stimulate its birth, yet clinical supervision remains largely in the womb. Perhaps though, and hopefully so, its promised emergence is near.[1]

The valiant efforts toward which it speaks continue, with increasing fervor, in the hope that to include CS more securely in the instructional improvement repertory will indeed become a workable reality. In our (and our colleagues') work with schools, we see some emergence. And we feel good about the emergence of positive collaborative efforts to better schools in general.

Instructional and clinical supervision programs should receive strong support from the administration of the school district, and they should be considered one of the most important of all funded efforts in the district. But instructional and clinical supervision has not yet been appropriated a major slot in the organization of schools, and the question of whether it belongs in administration or curriculum has not been answered adequately enough to get instructional improvement progressing as it should.

Many school personnel are maintenance-oriented; together with role discrepancies, that creates problems for clinical supervisors and instructional supervision programs. Instructional improvement efforts could be increased if supervisors received more support and allotted time.

In any CS effort, staff development must be the key. Observation and analysis of teaching by supervisors must exist for the purpose of instructional improvement, not evaluation. The survey results of teacher, principal, and supervisor views of CS as reported in Chapter 1 are encouraging. We invite the reader to review them.

THE SUPERVISOR'S ROLE

■ In Chapter 2, we discussed qualities for successful supervisor leadership. In Chapter 3, we discussed the role of teaming in clinical supervision. And throughout the text we have emphasized the collegiality and human resource development role in CS. We wish to reemphasize here the coaching role in collegial development. In education, peer coaching is becoming more and more popular as a device for helping teachers (and others) to grow in skill and understanding. Partially metaphorical and partially in literal translation, the term *coaching* is used to suggest *the provision to a teacher or other school worker of assistance, instruction, advice, or counsel by a co-worker who occupies either a leadership role (e.g., supervisor, department head, team leader, expert consultant) or a coordinate role (e.g., fellow teacher).* The coaching literature is already rich in education, and often it appears within the larger rubrics of human resource development or staff development. Recently the Association for Supervision and Curriculum Development published a volume of readings, taken from *Educational Leadership*, with the title "Coaching and Staff Development" (Brandt, 1989). The dimensions of the topic are reflected in sections titled "Building a Culture for Professional Growth," "Research on Teaching," "Research in Staff Development," "Collegiality," and "Coaching." We feel, as we have tried to stress in this volume, that coaching is integral to CS. By making it so, we believe that we will take a gigantic step from conception to emergence in the world of public education. *We cannot overemphasize the collegial role of CS for today and for the future.*

RAPPORT AND MUTUAL TRUST

■ The table opening this chapter indicates only one word to describe the role of rapport and mutual trust in CS: crucial. In Chapter 4 we discussed the importance of setting the stage for CS. Rapport and rapport nurturance is integral to not only preparing for, but also implementing, CS. *Rapport, a harmonious relationship with and between people, requires a knowledge base built upon a foundation of theory in administration and supervision.* In Chapter 4, we presented ideas of key theorists in motivation and positive view of self for that necessary knowledge base. And we examined rapport largely under the assumption that clinical supervisors have the necessary personal strength both to merit teacher confidence and respect and to cope with the stress of persons with a low self-concept whom they occasionally encounter. *Rapport is a constant throughout the CS process, a necessary ingredient without which we cannot begin to effect instructional improvement. Mutual trust must be a continual, conscious process. It necessitates use of human-relations skills, in appropriate degrees, and with appropriate timing.*

LITERATURE EMPHASIS

Through 1980

Robert Goldhammer's 1969 text *Clinical Supervision: Special Methods for the Supervision of Teachers*,[2] of which this book is a third edition, was the first major text on clinical supervision. Two others were completed within the next few years, both of which (like Dr. Goldhammer's) grew out of experiences in the Harvard-Newton and Harvard-Lexington programs. In 1971, Richard Weller wrote *Verbal Communication in Instructional Supervision*,[3] a text that grew out of his Harvard doctoral dissertation and examined the definition and practice of CS. In it, he developed an observational category system for analysis of teaching, Multidimensional Observational System for the Analysis of Interactions in Clinical Supervision, or MOSAICS. In 1973, Cogan's *Clinical Supervision*[4] provided a rationale for the use of CS as well as a full description of the process. His text is concerned with both CS setting and practice. Of the three texts that grew out of the work at Harvard, both Cogan's and Goldhammer's books are considered milestones—each in its own distinctive style and content. Cogan, the mentor, delivered a precise, well-documented CS text. Goldhammer, the student, offered a freewheeling, yet deep-thinking, personal analysis and description of the CS method, with an impassioned plea for its use in schools. Both served their purposes well.

No other major works on clinical supervision appeared in texts or as issue themes of journals until 1976. Bellon et al. produced a CS version in the text *Classroom Supervision and Instructional Improvement*.[5] In that same year, the winter issue of *Journal of Research and Development in Education*[6] featured the theme of clinical supervision. That issue, guest-edited by Robert Krajewski with featured articles by Cogan, Flanders, Frymier, Harris, Krajewski, McCleary, Sergiovanni, and Shane, is even today referred to as "the Bible of periodical literature on clinical supervision." Also in 1976, Abraham Fischler (another former Harvard faculty member) wrote a chapter in Louis Rubin's text *Improving In-Service Education: Proposals and Procedures for Change*[7] titled "Confrontation: Changing Teacher Behavior Through Clinical Supervision." In it, he emphasized data acquisition for the teacher via videotape and audiotape to enable the teacher to become a partner in the improvement process. The Fall 1977 issue of *Contemporary Education*[8] also featured CS as the theme. In 1978, Reavis produced a Phi Delta Kappa "Fastback" on CS.[9] In 1980, ASCD published *Clinical Supervision: A State of the Art Review*,[10] a short monograph by Cheryl Sullivan, a doctoral student. Also in 1980, the second edition of Goldhammer's text (with Robert Anderson and Robert Krajewski as co-authors) was completed.[11]

These works rank as the most scholarly and comprehensive on CS—in text and journal issue theme format. Still other texts mention CS and afford some ideas on the topic. Mosher and Purpel, in their text *Supervision: The Reluctant Profession*,[12] devote a chapter to a realistic appraisal of CS. Fred Wilhelms, in an ASCD publication, *Supervision in a New Key*,[13] also provided CS information in a separate chapter of his monograph. He declared that CS "is not so much supervision in a new key as it is traditional supervision with full orchestration and with every instrument finely tuned." Too, Blumberg[14] pointed to the CS method in his texts. In 1980, Keith Acheson and Meredith Gall produced *Techniques in the Clinical Supervision of Teachers*,[15] with a second edition in 1987.

1981 Through the Present

In preparing for this chapter, we explored about 20 supervision textbooks published since approximately 1982 for references to clinical supervision. In about half, there is either no mention of the topic or at most one or two pages within which there is acknowledgement or mention of either the Goldhammer five-stage cycle or the Cogan eight-stage cycle, or both. On the other hand, several of the most recent volumes do contain sections, or even chapters, in which CS is examined in some detail.

As is recognized in nearly all of the recent writings about CS, and especially the related phenomena for which terms such as *peer supervision*, *peer coaching*, *mentoring*, *tutoring*, and *collegial assistance* are being used, helping teachers to assume greater responsibility for improving their own as well as colleagues' instructional skills is now seen as a high priority in American schools. One of the best statements about "colleagueship in supervision" was provided by Alfonso and Goldsberry in the 1982 ASCD yearbook.[16] These scholars note that there must exist a larger, ongoing, comprehensive plan for instructional improvement if efforts at peer supervision or CS are to be productive. They observe, however, that teachers usually work in isolation and very little feedback on teaching performance is usually provided within the minimal supervision that exists, so that colleagueship efforts probably will provide a form of help that is not available elsewhere.

In a chapter prepared for the landmark ASCD yearbook *Supervision of Teaching*,[17] Garman provides an especially thoughtful overview of clinical supervision. An associate of both Cogan and Goldhammer during the years when the University of Pittsburgh was the intellectual and operational headquarters of clinical supervision, Garman traces the evolution of CS (including, in a footnote, the etymology of the term *clinical* back to the seventeenth century), examines the knowledge base, constructs, and concepts of supervision, and then develops the concepts of collegiality and collaboration. Hers is a call for depth and richness in the interactions that CS stimulates.

Lovell and Wiles[18] provide a 14-page chapter about clinical supervision, in which concepts, assumptions, and the process of CS are detailed. The authors assert a strong belief in CS as a system for helping, supporting, and providing services to teachers.

Tanner and Tanner[19] open their discussion of CS with reference to its Harvard origins, and in doing so credit Harvard's president James B. Conant with proposals as early as 1936 for bringing pre-service teacher education to the graduate level, where "a coherent theoretical-research base [could serve] as a guide for intelligent practice."

They also mention Conant's 1963 proposal that "the supervision of students in the practice-teaching phase of their preparation be conducted under the direction of the clinical professor whose status would be 'analogous to that of a clinical professor in certain medical schools.'" The "clinical professor" in this proposal would be a highly skilled and experienced classroom teacher who also holds rank as a university professor. The analogy to medicine, in Conant's mind, derived from the view that the developing sciences undergirding instructional practice are no less complex or important than the developing sciences that undergird medicine, and the clinical professors in both instances serve as intermediaries between the basic sciences and the future practitioner.

In a particularly important book in the field of supervision, by Sergiovanni and Starratt,[20] a thoughtful chapter, 35 pages long, examines "Clinical Supervision and Teacher Evaluation." The authors state at the outset that "since clinical supervision in all its forms involves making informal judgements about teaching, teacher evaluation is inevitably involved in the process." They go on to acknowledge that teachers generally disdain evaluation, and therefore disdain supervision, which, they believe, is a term to "hide" evaluation.

Within the chapter, CS is defined as a "partnership in inquiry" and an "in-class support system." "The heart of clinical supervision is an intense, continuous, mature relationship between supervisors and teachers with the intent being the improvement of professional practice." The platform concept is then discussed in relationship to CS, it being noted teachers sometimes are unaware of the contradiction that there may be between the espoused platform and assumptions, beliefs, and theories that actually guide their classroom decisions and behavior.

Beach and Reinhartz[21] have a brief seven-page section on CS within a chapter on "Models of Supervision." In addition to reviewing the "Goldhammer Five-Step Process," they attach a figure in which the five stages circulate around a core labelled "Formative Evaluation of Teaching Episode" and are surrounded by a circle indicating that formative assessment procedures are based on what is known about effective teaching. This, we perceive, is a succinct and appropriate description of the cycle.

Daresh[22] includes a 16-page chapter in which are presented underlying assumptions: developing an appropriate climate, stages of the clinical supervision cycle, and limits of CS. The general tone of the chapter is supportive, but the author observes that CS's "use in a school is always contingent upon the extent to which a climate of openness and trust exists in that school between supervisors and teachers. The model may be used only when teachers and supervisors share a fundamental respect for each other."

The most extensive discussion of CS appears in Peter Oliva's third edition of *Supervision in Today's Schools*,[23] which has a 36-page chapter on the topic. This is the longest and most comprehensive CS chapter in any of the texts.

In the second edition of his highly respected textbook, Glickman[24] devotes 11 pages to discussion of clinical supervision, as part of a chapter on "Direct Assistance to Teachers." Included in the discussion is commentary on coaching, seen as a peer use of CS, in which it is emphasized that for peer supervision to be successful there need to be, in addition to agreement and voluntarism, components addressing the purpose of the coaching, the training that participants require, the scheduling provision of necessary time, and various monitoring activities including troubleshooting. In summary, Glickman notes that failure to provide CS and other forms of assistance gives a very wrong message to teachers, to the effect that their work is unimportant and an isolated life ("Keep your doors shut and your problems to yourself") is good enough.

Other Sources After 1982

It is no longer possible for the ordinary scholar or practitioner to keep up with the flow of AERA (American Educational Research Association) papers, conference reports, monographs, association publications, agency leaflets, and convention handouts in which the topic of CS is being addressed. Articles published about CS or aspects thereof in the professional literature, especially in the two journals sponsored by ASCD (*Educational Leadership* and notably the *Journal of Curriculum and Supervision*) over the past decade have been numerous, valuable, and thought-provoking. We may safely assume that CS in its many dimensions has been intellectually revisited time and time again.

Without intent to slight the other contributors to this expanding literature, we observe that much of the material has come from those scholars whose work is reviewed earlier in this chapter, and from professors who participate actively in the Council of Professors of Instructional Supervision. Another large segment comes from practitioners in the public schools, sometimes in collaboration with university-based colleagues, reporting their experiences with a CS approach. While it is dangerous to generalize, it seems that the periodical literature is gradually enlarging upon the textbook discussions, enriching them through more in-depth analysis while also providing more concrete descriptions of CS at work.

Efforts to pull data searches together are sometimes complicated by the fact that CS is also a label in general use in the field of counseling psychology, as well as in the so-called Hunter Model of CS, which surely has much merit but which in our view is too authoritarian (there is no teacher-initiated "contract") to fit within our Cogan/Goldhammer-oriented definition. Another complication, although a welcome one, is that some closely related ideas and procedures are described within the literatures of coaching, mentoring, collegial assistance, and other terms that the computer fails to recognize as kindred to CS. However, we are delighted that in the 1990s there is so much being said, not only in books but in all sorts of publications, about the "arranged interactions" that focus upon in-class teacher behaviors.

OBSERVATION METHODOLOGY

■ Supervision has long been criticized for its lack of objectivity; unfortunately that criticism has some foundation. In Chapter 6, we identified four modes of recording data: audiotape, written records, videotape, and objective instrumentation. Objective analysis systems are the most desirable of the four, but we recommend they be supplemented by taping and creative note-taking. More than 100 objective analysis systems are available for classroom use for measuring various criteria. As teacher specialization increases, the need for objectivity in analysis becomes even greater. In pre-observation conferences, the teacher and supervisor determine which foci should be observed and in what objective manner they are to be observed. Teachers prefer an objective instrument that is practical and simple to use and interpret, one that they may eventually be able to self-administer. In Chapter 6 we presented three such instruments for the reader to learn about and use in supervisory observation: Flanders Interaction Analysis Category (FIAC), Behavior-Based Observation (BBO), and Teacher Question Index (TQI). Instrument use can be reinforced by videotape and other means, as depicted by the cyclical model presented in Chapter 6. Instrumentation can also be used to analyze the supervisor's behavior performance, and in Chapter 9 we present a strong rationale for its use in post-conference analysis.

SUMMARY: TOWARD THE FUTURE

■ As depicted in the table opening this chapter, clinical supervision has made measurable strides over the past two decades in emphasis (through synthesis of method and concepts, in use in schools, in supervisor role, and in rapport and mutual trust)—through more collegial emphasis, in literature emphasis (through individual and collective efforts of Council of Professors of Instructional Supervision members, both in their own organization and in ASCD), and in observation methodology (through increased use of objective analysis systems).

What type of people do supervisors supervise? A 1991 report by McGee et al,[25] in surveying a systematic sample of the Texas State Teachers Association membership, says the typical Texas teacher is married, has two children, is conservative, healthy, generally happy with self, doesn't drink or take drugs, favors corporal punishment, is not trained to work with mainstreamed children, lives within five miles of work, works in room during planning period, and prefers a male principal. Thus, in Texas at least (and, we surmise, throughout the remaining states in our country), supervisors typically work with teachers who are good models and good citizens who reflect a lot of the middle-class values so admired in our society. How should supervisors supervise them?

We see CS in the future as a business oriented toward professional growth, one built in a team framework with mutual assistance for mutually developed instructional improvement goals. We see CS as staff development, particularly a coaching form of staff development. Overall we view CS as human resource development. Several recent resources reaffirmed this view. John Smyth, in *Teachers as Collegial Learners: Challenging Dominant Forms of Supervision*,[26] notes that more and more teachers help each other and become collaborative learners. In his critique(s) of models of supervision, he approves of the collegial process used by and for teachers. Diane Dunlap and Paul Goldman, in a 1991 article "Rethinking Power in Schools," [27] describe facilitative power as *a process that allows subordinates to enhance their individual and collective performance.* Tomorrow's decision making will require even more collaboration between professionals whose expertise has less in common. CS, they claim, is consistent with current reform emphases and the earlier foci on effective schools and instructional leadership because CS is a facilitative system in which professional power is examined and actualized through others on the basis of trust and reciprocity.

Their statements complement our own, and vice versa. As we look to the future, then, we return to words which Robert Goldhammer wrote in the first edition of this book, and which remain true today:

> In its present stage of development, the CS that our minds can formulate and which we practice does not completely fulfill the ideology that occupies our imaginations. Day by day we know, better, what it is, in life and in professional life, that we're after. And by small increments, we are getting to know, better, how to get what we're after.
>
> The supervision we envisage is intended to increase teachers' incentives and skills for self-supervision and for supervising their professional colleagues. It is additionally intended to become progressively more useful as teachers become increasingly capable of employing it creatively.

> Our minds struggle for images of a supervision whose principal effect is to expand the sense of gratification experienced by students and teachers and supervisors, gratification in being and gratification in the work they do.
>
> The aims of CS will be realized when, largely by virtue of its own existence, everyone inside the school will know better why he/she is there, will want to be there, will be concerned with important curriculum questions, and will feel a strong and beautiful awareness of his/her own, individual identity and a community of spirit and enterprise with those beside him/her. [28]

These are the values that motivate our work and give rise to our ambitions. Although we cannot make promises that are as large as our dreams, we can proclaim those dreams and let ourselves be guided by them.

REFERENCES

[1] Robert J. Krajewski, Preface, *Journal of Research and Development in Education 9 (2)*, Winter 1976 (Theme: Clinical Supervision), University of Georgia, Athens.

[2] Robert Goldhammer, *Clinical Supervision: Special Methods for the Supervision of Teachers*, 1st ed., Holt, Rinehart and Winston, New York, 1969.

[3] Richard H. Weller, *Verbal Communication in Instructional Supervision: An Observational System for and Research Study of Clinical Supervision in Groups*, Teachers College Press, New York, 1971.

[4] Morris L. Cogan, *Clinical Supervision*, Houghton Mifflin, Boston, 1973.

[5] Jerry Bellon et al., *Classroom Supervision and Instructional Improvement*, Kendall/Hunt, Dubuque, Iowa, 1976.

[6] *Journal of Research and Development in Education 9 (2)*, Winter 1976 (Theme: Clinical Supervision), Robert J. Krajewski, ed., University of Georgia, Athens.

[7] Abraham S. Fischler, "Confrontation: Changing Teacher Behavior Through Clinical Supervision," in *Improving In-Service Education: Proposals and Procedures for Change*, Louis J. Rubin, ed., Allyn and Bacon, Boston, 1971.

[8] *Contemporary Education 49*, Fall 1977 (Theme: Clinical Supervision), Robert J. Krajewski, ed., Indiana State University, Terre Haute.

[9] Charles A. Reavis, *Teacher Improvement Through Clinical Supervision*, Phi Delta Kappa, Bloomington, Indiana, 1978.

[10] Cheryl Sullivan, *Clinical Supervision: A State of the Art Review*, Association for Supervision and Curriculum Development, Alexandria, Virginia, 1980.

[11] Robert Goldhammer, Robert H. Anderson, and Robert J. Krajewski, *Clinical Supervision, Special Methods for the Supervision of Teachers*, 2nd ed., Holt, Rinehart and Winston, New York, 1980.

[12] Ralph L. Mosher and David E. Purpel, *Supervision: The Reluctant Profession*, Houghton Mifflin, Boston, 1972.

[13] Fred T. Wilhelms, *Supervision in a New Key*, Association for Supervision and Curriculum Development, Washington, D.C., 1973.

[14] Arthur Blumberg, *Supervisors and Teachers: A Private Cold War*, McCutchan, Berkeley, California, 1974.

[15] Keith A. Acheson and Meredith Gall, *Techniques in the Clinical Supervision of Teachers: Preservice and Inservice Applications*, 2nd ed., Longman, New York, 1987.

[16] Robert J. Alfonso and Lee Goldsberry, "Colleagueship in Supervision," in *Supervision of Teaching* (1982 ASCD Yearbook), Thomas J. Sergiovanni, ed., Association for Supervision and Curriculum Development, Alexandria, Virginia, 1982.

[17] Noreen Garman, "The Clinical Approach to Supervision," in *Supervision of Teaching* (1982 ASCD Yearbook), Thomas J. Sergiovanni, ed., Association for Supervision and Curriculum Development, Alexandria, Virginia, 1982.

[18] John Lovell and Kimball Wiles, *Supervision for Better Schools*, 5th ed., Prentice-Hall, Englewood Cliffs, New Jersey, 1983.

[19] Daniel Tanner and Laurel Tanner, *Supervision in Education: Problems and Practices*, Macmillan, New York, 1987, pp. 180-181.

[20] Thomas J. Sergiovanni and Robert J. Starratt, *Supervision: Human Perspectives*, 4th ed., McGraw-Hill, New York, 1988.

[21] Don M. Beach and Judy Reinhartz, *Supervision: Focus on Instruction*, Harper and Row, New York, 1989.

[22] John C. Daresh, *Supervision as a Proactive Process*, Longman, New York, 1988, p. 230.

[23] Peter F. Oliva, *Supervision in Today's Schools*, 3rd ed., Longman, New York, 1988.

[24] Carl Glickman, *Supervision of Instruction: A Developmental Approach*, 2nd ed., Allyn and Bacon, Boston, 1990.

[25] Jerry McGee et al., *Profile of Texas Teachers: A Study of the Characteristics of Texas Teachers in 1990*, Sam Houston State University, Huntsville, Texas, September 1991.

[26] John Smyth, *Teachers as Collegial Learners: Challenging Dominant Forms of Supervision*, Open University Press, Buckingham, October 1991.

[27] Diane Dunlap and Paul Goldman, "Rethinking Power in Schools," in *Educational Administration Quarterly 1*, February 1991, pp. 5-29.

[28] See Note 2 above.

APPENDIX

The Clinical Supervision Cycle: An Overview

I. Pre-Observation Conference

A. Purposes
1. Confirm and nurture the teacher-supervisor relationship.
2. Identify teacher's needs and concerns, and develop means to address them.
3. Provide a conceptual rehearsal for lesson problem areas.
4. Ensure an agreement for rationale and method of observation.

B. Commentary. The pre-observation conference can:
1. Serve to relax both parties by setting the tone for the entire supervisory experience.
2. Help identify both long- and short-term teaching concerns.
3. Establish a shared decision-making climate for ground rules of the lesson to be observed.
4. Determine foci for observation.
5. Determine data-gathering instruments for lesson foci.

II. Observation

A. Purpose: Observe the lesson and obtain objective data on determined foci.

B. Commentary. In observation:
1. Carry out logistics of pre-observation as planned.
2. Observe objectively with instrumentation.
3. Be minimally distracting to students and teacher.

III. Analysis and Strategy

A. Purposes
1. Reconstruct observed events as objectively as possible.
2. Sort and relate these events to the determined foci.
3. Review data thoroughly, analyze noteworthy patterns of the teacher's behavior, and consider supervisory implications.
4. Plan a strategy for the conference.
5. Look ahead to future teacher growth and development.

B. Commentary. In analysis and strategy:
1. Focus on classroom data which matters most in the lives of children and teachers (saliency).

2. Concentrate on things about which something can be done (treatability).
3. Don't deal with too much at once. Choose only a few things on which it is possible for both the supervisor and teacher to concentrate on in a manageable way (selectivity).
4. Arrange data in understandable, usable, communicable form.
5. Postpone judgments until you establish an objective base from thorough data review.
6. Plan to work with strengths.
7. Settle on a strategy for conference opening.

IV. Supervision Conference

A. Purposes
   1. Define and confirm teaching issues through lesson feedback.
   2. Provide didactic help for improving future teaching.
   3. Provide training in techniques of teacher self-improvement.

B. Commentary. In the supervisory conference:
   1. Pre-arrange for logistic considerations.
   2. Promote a relationship of mutual trust and respect.
   3. Plan for opening, transition, and closing.
   4. Respond to teacher's perceived morale and state of mind.
   5. Be an exemplar of strategies espoused for the teacher.

V. Post-Conference Analysis

A. Purposes
   1. Reconstruct, as appropriate, the events of the conference.
   2. Assess the conference in terms of:
      a. Teacher's criteria, as determined in the pre-observation conference.
      b. Supervisory criteria.
      c. Apparent value of the conference to the teacher.
   3. Evaluate the supervisor's skill in handling the several stages of the cycle.

B. Commentary. Post-conference analysis can:
   1. Provide a basis for assessing whether supervision is working productively.
   2. Help participants understand better the intellectual and emotional dimensions of the teacher's work.

INDEX